ZIG+ZAG'S
DIRTY DEEDS DOSSIER

ANGELO ABELA

BOXTREE

ACKNOWLEDGEMENTS
Zig and Zag would like to thank the following people: Simon Wright, Analisa Baretto and all at Working Title; Ronan, Paula, Anne, Mike, Damien and all at Double Z Enterprises; Mike, Fran, Gerry, Chris, Pross, Sammy, Liz and Midge from the English TV crew, and Rob and Frankie from the American TV crew; and most of all Angelo Abela our Director and co-writer, who stayed up all hours to do this for us – which made him a stranger to his wife Caroline, his kids Lulu and Jack and his very good friends Mick and Ciaran.

First published in the UK in 1996 by Boxtree Limited,
Broadwall House, 21 Broadwall, London, SE1 9PL

Copyright © Double Z Enterprises 1996. Licensed by Copyright Promotions Ltd.

'Zig and Zag's Dirty Deeds' is a Working Title Television/
Double Z Enterprises Production for Channel 4

ISBN: 0 7522 0379 7

10 9 8 7 6 5 4 3 2 1

Design by Blackjacks
Colour reproduction by Scanners

This publication may not be reproduced, transmitted or held in a retrieval system in part or in whole in any form or using any electronic, mechanical, photocopying or recording process or any other process without the publisher having first given permission in writing. Except in the U.S.A., this book is sold subject to the condition that it shall not, by way of trade or otherwise, be lent, resold, hired out or otherwise circulated without the publisher's prior permission in any form of binding or cover other than that in which it is published and without a similar condition being imposed on a subsequent purchaser.

Printed and bound in Great Britain by Cambus Litho Ltd, East Kilbride.

A CIP catalogue entry for this book is available from the British Library

Picture credits:
Front cover: Double Z Enterprises. Back cover: Angela Nott: bottom left & middle. Stuart Freedman: bottom right. Working Title/Angelo Abela: top. All Action Pictures: 60 top; 61 bottom; 67 bottom; 75. Stuart Freedman: 12 right; 69. The Hulton Getty Picture Collection: 22; 84; 33. Ken Loveday: 26. Mary Evans Picture Library: 30; 31; 32. Michael Vine Associates: 24 top. Angela Nott: 1; 4 & 5; 8 & 9; 76 & 77; 69 bottom. Eddie Otchere: 15 bottom; 16. Retna Picture Library: 11; 12 left; 13 left & right; 23; 47 top & middle; 54; 60 right; 61 top; 84 middle & bottom; 84; 89 top. Rex Features: 36 bottom; 51. Working Title Television/Angelo Abela: 28 top; 37 bottom; 40 & 41; 44; 48; 52 & 53; 55; 57; 67; 70; 73; 87 bottom; 93; 94 bottom. Working Title Television/ Double Z Enterprises/Channel 4: 15 top & middle; 19; 24 bottom; 26 top; 28 middle & bottom; 35; 39; 42; 43; 45; 46; 56; 58; 64; 65 middle & bottom; 66; 68 top three; 79; 80; 81; 82; 83; 87 top; 88 bottom; 90; 91; 92; 94 top; 95. All other photographs: Double Z Enterprises.

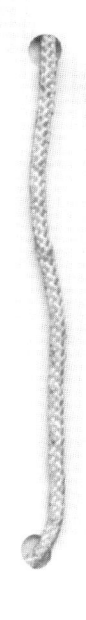

"You pay, we prey"

contents

Pledge of Allegiance — 4
Dirty Deeds Applications Forms — 6
Dos and Don'ts of a Dirty Deeder — 8
Dirty Deeds File 001 – "Gingerella" — 10
Secretaries Application Form — 18
Typical Secretaries — 19
Ideal Secretaries — 20
Dirty Deeds File 002 – "Comic Collision" — 22
Dirty Deeds in History — 30
Dirty Deeds File 003 – "Desperately Seeking Swimming Trunks" — 34
Dirty Deeds File 004 – "Still Desperately Seeking Swimming Trunks" — 46
Dirty Deeds We're Not Allowed to Show — 60
Dirty Deeds File 005 – "Battle of the Bands" — 62
ZigCams — 70
Dirty Deeds File 006 – "This Party Sucks" — 74
Dirty Deeds We'd Like to Do — 84
Dirty Deeds File 007 – "To Elle and Back" — 86

in yer face, mizzuz

fun thiz way →

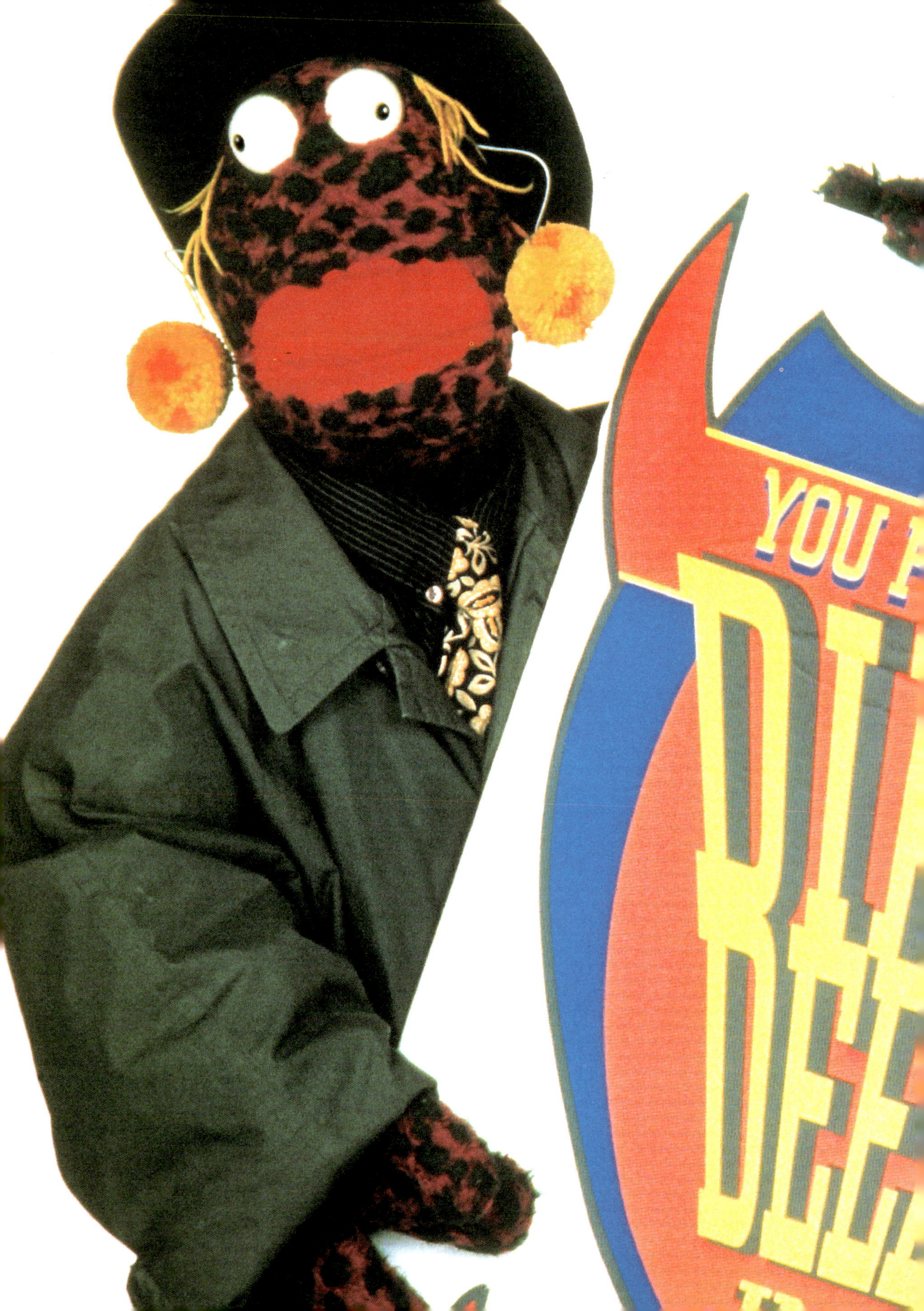
YOU

We, the undersigned, do hereby pledge allegiance to the Dirty Deed Badge. Promising that everything will be done in an underhand way, and that all aspects of Dirty Deeding be kept very hush hush, 'cos we don't want everyone doing it, do we? I also promise that all the money that I earn as a Dirty Deeder will go directly to Zag's personal bank account. If I end up owing money ... ask Zig.

Signed Zig   Zag

DIRTY DEED AGENT NO. 1

NAME Zagnatious Hillary Zogly
AGE 18ft 19in
HEIGHT 3ft 11in
WEIGHT Get lost
EYES Yes
HAIR Titian
FUR Purple with green beauty spots
DISTINGUISHING MARKS Lipstick traces from various babes
QUALIFICATIONS Look I'm famous – O.K.!!
OCCUPATIONS WITHIN PAST 5 YEARS TV Alien Love God and heartbreaker of a million models' hearts
HOBBIES Round the world yacht racing, clubbing
FAVE FOOD Peschwari Nan
FAVE DRINK Zoga Cola
FAVE BAND Dog Eat Dog and Terrorvision
FAVE PERSON Jeremy Paxman
FAVE SPORT Snowboarding
FAVE INANIMATE OBJECT Celine Dion
FAVE BROTHER Me
PERSONAL MOTTO I'm Great!
DIRTY DEED I WOULD MOST LIKE TO DO The "Bon Jovi must not act again" Deed sent in by all people who like to go to the cinema

AUTHORISED BY Me

DIRTY DEED AGENT NO. 2

NAME Zigmund Ambrose Zogly
AGE 14ft
HEIGHT 3ft 11in
WEIGHT Wait where?
EYES Two
HAIR Green
FUR Yes, even between my toes
DISTINGUISHING MARKS Mark Little, Mark from Take That
QUALIFICATIONS My brother does that stuff OK!
OCCUPATIONS WITHIN PAST 5 YEARS I have been on telly on Earth with my brother, his name is Zag
HOBBIES Lego and car rubbings
FAVE FOOD Fish fingers
FAVE DRINK Fish fingers
FAVE BAND The Fish Finger Band
FAVE PERSON My dad - Jeremy Clarkson from Top Gear
FAVE SPORT Dog bowling
FAVE INANIMATE OBJECT Wallace and Gromit
FAVE BROTHER Zag
PERSONAL MOTTO In yer face, missus!
DIRTY DEED I WOULD MOST LIKE TO DO Whatever my brother does tell me to do because he says he the "boss of me"

AUTHORISED BY Zag

DOS AND DON'TS OF A DIRTY DEEDER

ZAG

DO ANY JOB THAT IS WELL PAID. (Money must always be paid up front as well – CASH!)

DO ANYTHING THAT NEEDS FOR THE DEED TO BE DONE, THE DIRTIER THE BETTER. (If this includes bending the law a little then so be it. Remember my motto – A Rolling Stone shouldn't be still doing concerts. It's criminal – and if they can get away with it, why can't I?)

DO ALWAYS TRY TO COME UP WITH YOUR OWN DIRTY DEED WHILST ON A MISSION. (See the two LA shows where I not only pinched the Baywatch costumes as requested but kidnapped the Baywatch cast as well.)

DO TRY TO SURROUND YOURSELF WITH BABES. (This won't help the case, but it will mean that you'll have someone to snog while you send Zig off on an errand.)

DON'T RISK YOUR OWN SKIN FOR A DIRTY DEED. (Always send Zig into these situations – see point made above.)

do be do be...

ZIG

DO EAT ALL YOUR BROCCOLI (Or if you don't Broccoli boy will come and get you. He's got a particularly nasty way of making people do what he wants them to. It involves holding them underneath a duvet and passing wind – flatulence is one of the many wonderful and amusing side effects of broccoli eating.)

DO WATCH ANYTHING THAT HAVE ZIG AND ZAG ON IT. (Look out for "Good Morning with Zig and Zag" – a show where we bore everyone rigid, well if Anne and Nick can do it, why can't we? Also coming is "Zogly's Behaving Badly", "The Zig and Zag Files" and "Eastenders" where Zag has an affair with every woman in the square, including Pat! And Zig turns the Queen Vic into a Broccoli bar.)

DO DO BE DO BE DO BE DO (Try to sing like Frank Sinatra not Frank Skinner and Dave Baddiel!)

DON'T EVER MAKE THE MISTAKE OF BELIEVING THAT ZIG IS A PERFECT COMIC CREATION THAT BLENDS CHILDISH INVENTIVENESS, SURREAL GENIUS AND SLAPSTICK SPLIT SECOND TIMIIING (Cos I'm not. I'm just plain Zig with no tongue, no nose and a nifty line of anoraks.)

ZIG AND ZAG'S DIRTY DEEDS FILE 001 "GINGERELLA"

TOP NON-SECRET

As dictated by Zig and Zag to secretary of the week, Miss Plumley

It was the first day of the rest of my life.

What's that supposed to mean? Isn't today the first day of the rest of your life?

Shut up, Zig! I was trying for an opening sentence that would strike a chord, mean something and be remembered as a classic opening line for generations to come.

How about, "It was the second day of the rest of my life. The first was spent laughing at Fergie's large overdraft and even bigger bottom"? Now that's an opening line!

Zig, if I needed help, I would ask for it, and were I to need it, which I don't, I certainly wouldn't ask someone that thinks that the best piece of literature is David Icke's biography ...

But it's the best piece of comedy writing ever.

... Well I don't need your advice, so please stop interrupting me, I'm trying to do the first daily report on our first ever Dirty Deeds case.

Oh okay, I'll just go off and get some Broccoli tea.

It was the ~~kick~~ ... the second day of the rest of my life. The first was spent cavorting with a beautiful babe on the beach in Barbados. Gentlemanly conduct (and her lawyer) forbids me from telling who she was ... let's just say that a certain one-time star of Baywatch ("Don't call me babe!") allowed me to find out if those things in her costume were natural bouyancy aids or not!

I think Fergie's bum is funnier.

SHUT UP! GO, GET YOUR BROCCOLI TEA!!

Anyway, what ever day it was in the rest of my life, today was the day that I became Dirty Deed agent No. 1. One of the proudest days of my life, not just because I was the first agent, but because this baby was all my idea. I'd had the idea a while ago, when my good friend and showbiz chum Sean Connery came to me and asked if I could get Timothy Dalton to stop playing James Bond, (Roger Moore was bad enough, but Dalton, this was just a joke). I pulled a few strings, paid a few corrupt stagehands and hired a particularly objectionable woman who pretended to be the world's biggest Bond fan. She threatened him with undying love, her knickers through the post and the odd confrontation with any other woman that dared to go out with Timothy Dalton ... Dalton didn't stand a chance, he soon folded.

Sean offered me some money, but I declined, after all he was a mate, and besides I'd used his Aston Martin on a date with Kim Basinger and she went wild as I whispered sweet nothings in her ear. She made a grab for me, missed, pulled on the steering wheel and totalled the car.

Sorry, I spilled some tea!

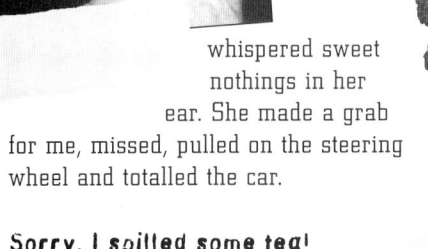

But it got me thinking. There must be thousands of my showbiz friends who need something done, but can't be seen doing it. And who better to pay big money than my showbiz friends? And who better to do those underhand Dirty Deeds (hence the name) for said vast amounts of money? An alien with no scruples ... ME! (Obviously if it's very dangerous then Zig can do it.) And that's why on the third day of the rest of my life – the first was spent canoodling with a certain Mrs. Lee, the second was spent laughing at Fergie's bum – I came to be sitting in the new Dirty Deeds office. Zig had 17 cups of Broccoli tea and I sat there picking up the phone every two minutes to see if it was still working. The sure-fire, success-waiting-to-happen, brilliant money-spinner, Dirty Deeds ... was a failure.

But it was cool, I got a swivel chair.

No-one wanted a Dirty Deed doing and so before I threw myself from the window on the twenty second floor, Zig suggested we go and get something to eat. He was obviously trying to get my mind off the depressing state the Dirty Deeds office was in.

Er, no, statistically people who jump from windows bounce better if they have a big lunch.

Well anyway, no-one wanted a Dirty Deed and so we went to the local cafe and tried to drown our sorrows in soup ...

Broccoli naturally.

But we got a shock ...

NO BROCCOLI SOUP!! What kind of establishment was this!

Besides that. An even bigger shock ...

Impossible.

Our waiter was none other than the GINGER WHINGER!

No, not that Ginger Whinger, the other one ...

CHRIS EVANS !

Saviour of Channel 4, Radio 1 and an island in the Pacific Islands. Chris was doing a part-time job there ...

Rubbish! He got the sack everywhere else. He had nowhere else to go.

That's not nice, Zig. Besides he may want us for another job, such as stapling Shaun Ryder's mouth together so that he can't swear on live TV again.

If we're going to staple mouths together, then my vote's for ENYA.

N.B. Send picture of Shaun with staples to Chris. See if he wants another Dirty Deed.

Anyway, Chris wanted, no NEEDED, something done. Something to get him back on top. He knew what it was ... drum

Drrrrrrrrrrrrrrrrrrrrrrrrrrrrrrrrrrrrrrrrrrrrrrrrrrrrr...

"GINGERELLA": a funny musical version of his life story.

Stapling Enya's mouth would get more laughs.

It was a job! A Dirty Deed! HURRAH, HURRAH, HOSANNA, HOSANNA, HOSANNA HEY! And all that malarkey. All we had to was find a theatre, get a cast, build the sets, do the advertising, get an audience and make sure it was a sell out.

What were we going to do in the afternoon?

Don't be cheeky! We had to do this because, for the first and last time I agreed not to take cash up front (see Zag's "Dos and Don'ts of a Dirty Deeder"), but to take a split of the box office. We had to make the show work otherwise Dirty Deeds would be bankrupt before we even got started.

We should never have taken a job from someone with red hair.

Finding a theatre proved to be a little harder than we thought. Most theatres are full, so we decided to get one of the shows that's already on, off.

ZIG + ZAG'S DIRTY DEEDS DOSSIER

N.B. Send a Dirty Deed flyer to the Liberal Democrats asking if they want anything done. They could certainly do with it.

As clear as mud. What Zag's trying to say is that we were going to sabotage the West End, causing chaos, panic, destruction and perhaps the overthrow of the government.

Sabotage, yes. Overthrow the government that's something else..

Here's a list of the shows we wanted to sabotage and how we were going to do it:

OLIVER
— Put laxatives into their gruel. Then the show would really run and run.

CATS
— Let a dog loose on the stage. Watch them trying to sing while a rottweiler chases the actors around.

STARLIGHT EXPRESS
— Derail the trains, or throw the wrong kind of leaves on the track.

MISS SAIGON
— Kidnap the lead actress, then Miss Saigon would miss the show.

GREASE
— Grease the brakes on the car and let it slide into the audience!

Why didn't we just blow one of the theatres up?

Sure Zig, then where would we have put the show on? Perhaps we could have blown up the theatre, then overnight got all the goblins and elves to help us rebuild it?

Now you're being silly ... we would have just asked the Fairy of Theatreland.

Zig, that is a set up for a cheap gag and I will not give the punchline, no matter how much I want to.

No, Zag, we saw the Theatre Fairy on stage. She was pretty and ...

Zig, I hate to be the one to break all of your illusions but that was Gaby Roslin in a costume.

Huh? You mean Gaby's a magical Fairy of the Theatre?

Forget it, Zig. Anyway we got the theatre (from Fairy Gaby, okay Zig?), and held open auditions. We got some very strange types coming (actors are pretty strange anyway) but these were really weird — American Indian impersonators, Elvis impersonators, gorilla impersonators, we even got a Keith Chegwin impersonator.

Someone impersonates Chegwin. That's sad!

Well, no, actually. The person impersonating Chegwin was actually Chegwin himself. It turns out that Chegwin auditioned five times in various disguises …

I thought he was great as the ballerina.

While dressed as the gorilla Chegwin somehow managed to get the part of Chris Evans in "Gingerella". Chris Evans thought he would be playing himself in the show, but Zig soon quickly put him right about that.

I told him he stank.

Keith threw himself into the part, he only had one day to learn the lines and make the set (that was part of the deal), but he did brilliantly.

Is Chegwin playing Chris Evans or Virgil from Thunderbirds?

WAHEY, WAHEY,
   A SYMBOL OF SEX,
WAHEY, WAHEY,
   WITH MY BLACK-RIMMED SPECS,
WAHEY, WAHEY,
   IT'S A WONDERFUL FABULOUS DAY.

AIN'T GONNA BE NO CHARLADY,
GONNA BE A STAR LADY.

I'LL THROW AWAY THIS BROOM, YOU
   CAN SWEEP YOUR OWN DAMN ROOM,
I'M CHRIS EVANS,
   I'M GINGER FISH FINGER.

I'M ME.

I still think they should have kept in that line...

"He's a great mate is Chris, His butt, Russ and Jono should kiss."

Chris came for the last ten minutes. He was so sure that the show was going to be a success that he had already quit his job as a waiter. We all listened in to the last big musical number and were overwhelmed at the standing ovation that it got. It was good though ... I wrote it!

But what we didn't know was that Chris had got other plans. After the show the Ginger Whinger ran off with the money!!

This is what Zag looked like when I told him about Chris.

Only more handsome obviously.

Well ...

Zig do you want a Chinese burn on your eyeball again? No, then **SHUT UP**.

Where was I? Oh yes, we heard from Evans later that week, he sent us a postcard from Barbados! I was ready to burst until I saw what was attached to the card ...

Aaaaaaaaaaaaaaaaaaaaaaaaaaaaaargh!

Bloyds Bank
EALING BRANCH
45 The Broadway Ealing London W5 5JU

PAY Dirty Deeds
Lots and lots and lots and lots and lots

APPLICATION FORM:- DIRTY DEEDS SECRETARY

NAME ....
AGE .... HEIGHT .... WEIGHT ....
EYES .... HAIR ....
DISTINGUISHING FEATURES ....
....
QUALIFICATIONS ....
....
PREVIOUS OCCUPATIONS ....
....
....

ALL QUESTIONS IN THIS SECTION MUST BE ANSWERED

ZAG'S QUESTIONS

STATISTICS .... (PLEASE SEND PHOTO IN BIKINI)

WOULD YOU KISS AN ALIEN? ☐ ☐ (If no, please stop now)
                                    YES NO

DO YOU LIKE DISCOS? ☐ ☐ ROMANTIC DINNERS? ☐ ☐ ME? ☐ ☐
                     YES NO   YES NO   YES NO

(If you answer no to any of the above, your application cannot be taken further)

PLEASE COMPLETE THE FOLLOWING TRUE STATEMENT:
I THINK ZAG IS FANTASTICALLY ATTRACTIVE BECAUSE ....
....
....
....
....
....

(Please finish answer on spare paper)

ZIG'S QUESTION IGNORE THIS SECTION

WHAT IS YOUR BEST BROCCOLI RECIPE
....

A FRUITY ASSORTMENT OF DIRTY DEEDS SECRETARIES

Miss Disco Diva
I don't think Disco was her real name, but it didn't matter. She could type at 150 bpm!

Miss L'Amour
I'll never forget Miss L'Amour, but I'll never forgive her either... running away with that bloomin' washboard tummied bunch!

Miss Barren
Miss Barren made an excellent cup of Broccoli tea.

ZIG + ZAG'S DIRTY DEEDS DOSSIER
SHEET 20 OF 96

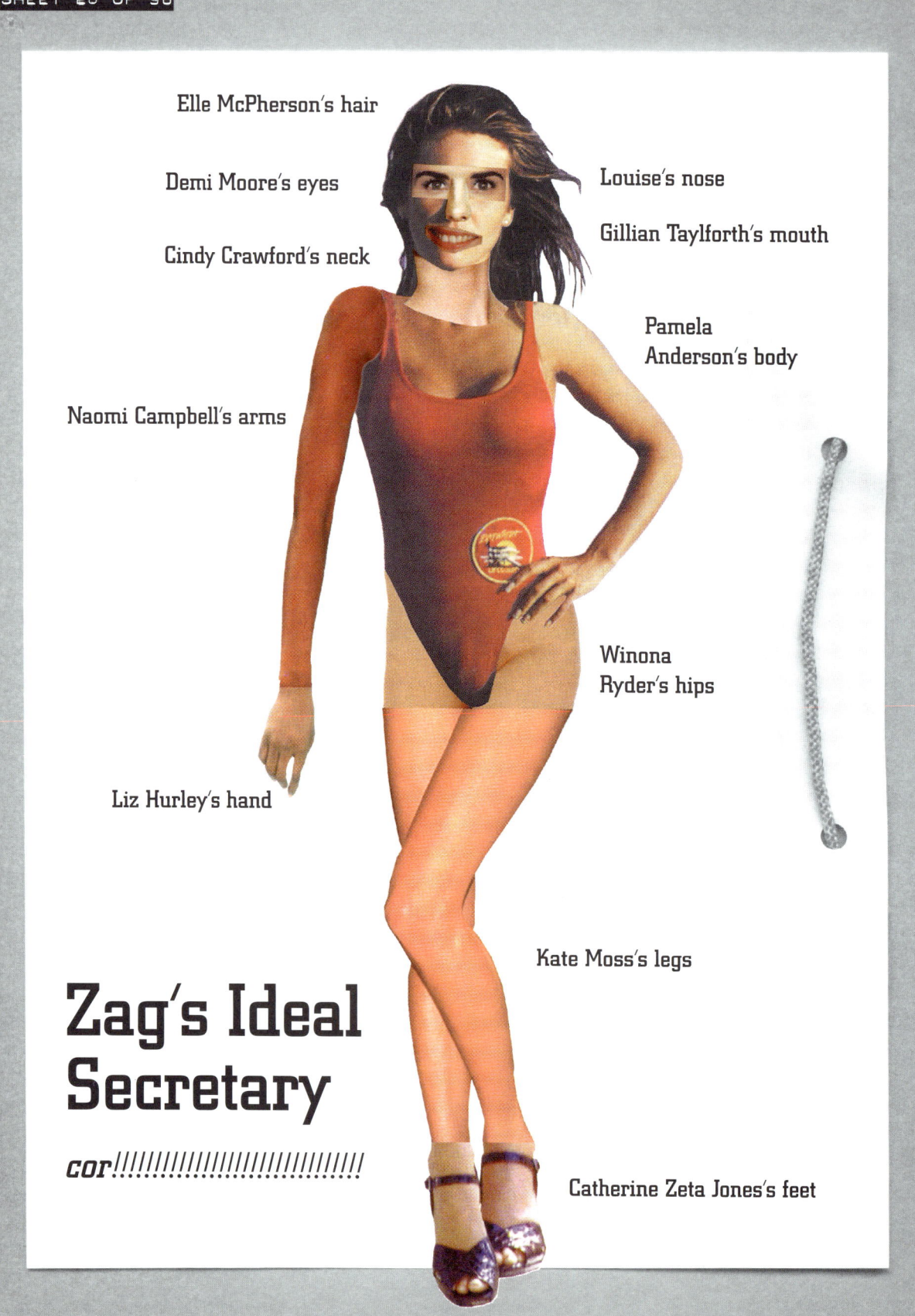

SECRETARY

Elle McPherson's hair

Demi Moore's eyes

Cindy Crawford's neck

Louise's nose

Gillian Taylforth's mouth

Pamela Anderson's body

Naomi Campbell's arms

Winona Ryder's hips

Liz Hurley's hand

Kate Moss's legs

Zag's Ideal Secretary

cor!!!!!!!!!!!!!!!!!!!!!!!!!!!!!!!!!!

Catherine Zeta Jones's feet

ZIG + ZAG'S DIRTY DEEDS DOSSIER
SHEET 21 OF 96

SECRETARY

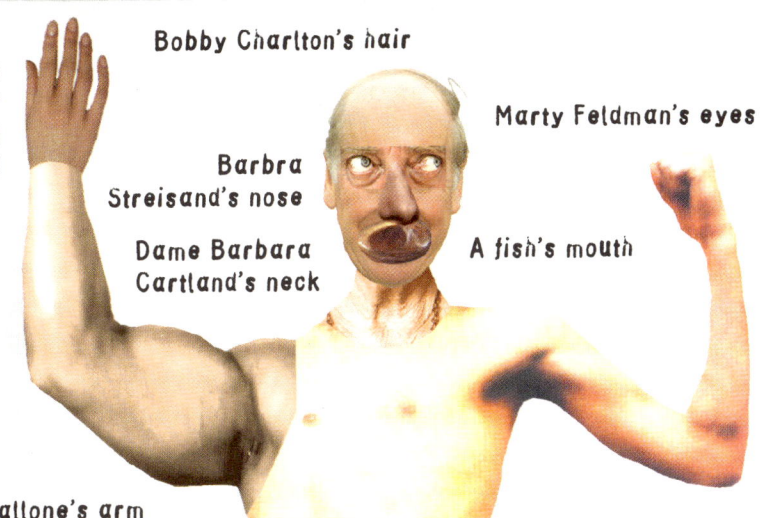

Bobby Charlton's hair

Delia Smith's hand for making broccoli food

Marty Feldman's eyes

Barbra Streisand's nose

Dame Barbara Cartland's neck

A fish's mouth

Stallone's arm

John Major's body

Timmy Mallett's hips

Danny De Vito's left leg

John Cleese's right leg

Zig's Ideal Secretary

ha ha ha ha ha ha ha ha ha ha ha ha

ZIG AND ZAG'S DIRTY DEEDS FILE 002 "COMIC COLLISION"

As dictated by Zig and Zag to secretary of the week, Miss Bottomoffsky

SECRETISH

After last week's pay off (see Dirty Deed 001 – "Gingerella"), the £100,000 lasted a whole week ...

Explain that to me again. Isn't £100,000 a lot of money?

Well no, not really, when you consider all of the expenses that we have had. Anyway, the Dirty Deeds office was getting a bit of a buzz about it ...

What expenses? £???????????????????

Well for example ... there was ... em ... the paper clips! We bought a lot of paper clips.

Are they very expensive?

Terribly. They cost over £100 each.

And what about your new car?

I had to buy that to get the paper clips back to the office safely. Can you imagine me getting back to the office by bus? I could have been mugged or anything. Satisfied now?

Okay ... but why have I got a bike?

I think it's important that you have some form of transport. We have to keep up appearances, don't we? It's all right, don't bother thanking me, I'll take the expense off your next wages.

I'm going to get paid for doing Dirty Deeds?

Well not money as such no, but you do get to drink all the Broccoli tea you can.

You're very good to me Zag. I'm going to get one now. Do you want one.

Thanks, but no thanks, I have to get on with dictating this Dirty Deed report.

Broccoli coffee? Broccoli milk shake? Broccoli sweater?

No, really, you have one if you want but I better get on with this otherwise we'll be onto our next Dirty Deed before we've done the report.

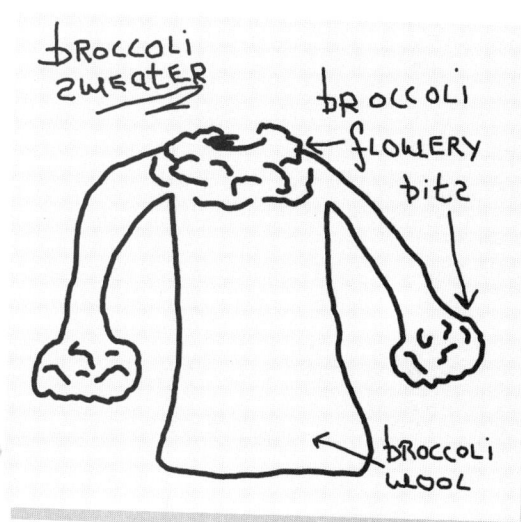

Anyway, I had managed to get the money to last a week and the buzz was going round. The ex-emperor of Tibet gave me a call and asked if we would try to get him his kingdom back, but I couldn't. He wanted it done on a certain date as foretold in the 4000-year-old scriptures, but I had a hot date with Catherine Zeta Jones and you have to get your priorities right.

JOE PASQUALE

We soon did however get a good job. Frank Carson sent a video tape in to us with a request for a Dirty Deed that I quite liked, it was to sort out a comic by the name of Joe Pasquale.

If you don't know who he is, he's the guy who sounds like Mickey Mouse on helium and looks like Danny Baker on diet pills and hair restorer.

The reason why Frank wanted him out of the picture was that Pasquale was favourite for winning the coveted GOLDEN MIKE AWARD, an award that went to the best comic doing a summer season in Blackpool. A bit of an oxymoron, I know ...

Isn't an oxymoron a stupid cow?

No, an oxymoron is something that doesn't go together, like sports and personality, or German and humour or Blackpool Summer Season and award winning comedy.

Or Broccoli and Custard?

Yes Zig, can I get on now? So that day we were on our way, I had fixed up with Zag Autos (a little side line I have going, our motto is "If you know of a better car, tell us where it is and we'll steal it!") for us to have a vehicle that would suit Blackpool, its people and the nightlife. This is what we got ...

I loved it. I could run over anybody I didn't like – traffic wardens, men just wearing T-shirts when it was -19°c, and especially anyone from the Broccoli Liberation Federation.

Shh Zig. We still haven't got that little fracas sorted out.

Zag, I refuse to take the blame for that incident. I saw some people wearing green and white scarves, the colours of the Broccoli Liberation Federation. How was I to know they were Celtic fans on a day out?

Zig, I understand that you see the BLF as an effrontery to life as we know it, you may be right, but that does not mean you can fire the tank at them, especially when they are standing on the Palace Pier.

What Palace Pier?

Exactly. A period pier of some historical note blasted out of the water because some people were wearing green and white. I ask you!

Good shot though.

So we were in Blackpool looking for Pasquale and it was proving more difficult than first thought. Very few people would tell us of his whereabouts, either because they were big fans and were covering up for him ...

Or they didn't know who the hell Pasquale was.

But we were determined to get our man. Dirty Deeders through and through, we always live up to our motto, don't we Zig?

Em, yes ... A broccoli in the hand gathers no moss.

... sometimes Zig, you're too stupid. If I didn't know you were my brother, I'd say that you must have come from a very stupid family. No, the Dirty Deed motto is ... *YOU PAY, WE PREY*.

That's prey as in the bird of prey, vulture-like, not pray as in get on your knees and shout HALLELUJAH!!

Thank you Zigmund. (For those of you that like to read quietly I apologise for my brother's outburst.) So, we're in Blackpool and we can't find Pasquale so we decide to find other ways to make sure that Carson wins the Golden Mike award:

- Buy all the Carson tickets and give them out FREE, so that Carson's theatre would be full as well.

BUT – we couldn't even give Carson's tickets away.

- Go up in a plane and throw the tickets out, thus making sure the tickets literally rained on the people below in some sort of publicity stunt.

BUT – the stunt went wrong and I fell out of the plane and landed on top of the Blackpool tower!

While at the top of the tower administering to my brother's wounds ...

You were not adminstering ... admiserining, administrating ... whatever ... to my wounds, you were causing them! You were jumping on my head for being so stupid as to fall out of the plane.

Yes well, while at the top of the tower, I came up with another wonderful plan: to turn off all the lights at the infamous Blackpool illuminations EXCEPT for the ones outside Carson's theatre, therefore ensuring that Carson's audience find their way to the theatre, AND that Pasquale's audience lose their way and fall into the sea. Brilliant.

If it was so brilliant, why didn't it work?

AHA! Well, yes. Now we come to the question, don't we. Aha! ... I have no idea. We managed to disguise ourselves as Pierce Brosnan and Antonio Banderas ... That went very well, we got to the very hub of the high-tech illuminations technical centre.

A room with a man testing light bulbs you mean?

I sidetracked him, talking about watts and volts, while you secretly turned off all the lights except for Carson's. But something went amiss, didn't it. You got carried away. Once you started shutting down lights, there was no stopping you. EVERY LIGHT IN THE WHOLE OF BLACKPOOL WENT OFF! It was so dark that no-one went to any theatres that night, they couldn't see where they were going. Buses crashed, a plane nearly went into the Blackpool tower and several hundred people wet themselves on the Big Dipper at Blackpool Pleasure Beach!

"ARE you Looking at me?"

Blackpool with no lights on

Huh, cool!

And we, may I remind you, had to walk home in the dark. I thought that I'd found a particularly soft trail of sand down by the beach. It was only when I got back to the hotel, and the lights were restored, that I realised that I had walked home along the donkey path.

They say that donkey doo is very good for the shoes, it makes them supple.

I wasn't wearing shoes, I thought that I was walking along the beach. I wanted to feel the sand squidge through my toes.

Urgh. I'm going to be sick!

While in bed that night, after giving my feet a good soak in the sink, Zig came up with the master plan to end all master plans.

We ice Pasquale ... make him worm food ... dance with him at club dead ... make him a reservation at Restaurant Hell ...

In other words we kill Pasquale!
After having that brainwave, Zig fell straight to sleep (thinking exhausts him), and then started making the oddest squawking noises in his sleep.

I was dreaming. It was really strange, me and Zag were in Las Vegas and we driving with these two showgirls, and singing them this song.

✯ OOH LAS VEGAS

*Ooh Las Vegas, it ain't Las Schmegas
It's my Las Vegas — One hell of a town!
Its got the lights, its got the sights
and ooh those crazy nights
Its got the girls, with the curls
and ooh those pretty girls
It's never closed, it never snows
and ooh heaven knows*

Zig, I know you think it was a dream and it was, but you have to remember that dream sequences still have to be filmed. We did actually go to Vegas, we did drive down the strip with those showgirls, we did gamble.

So you did lose $50,000.

Em ... no ... that was the only part of the dream sequence that you actually did dream.

I can never really get my head round all this filming lark, blurring reality and fantasy.

Luckily ... OK, so we got back from the dream sequence, and only had one last day to sort out Pasquale. We decided to plant an explosive device in his dressing room, and ice him at the theatre.

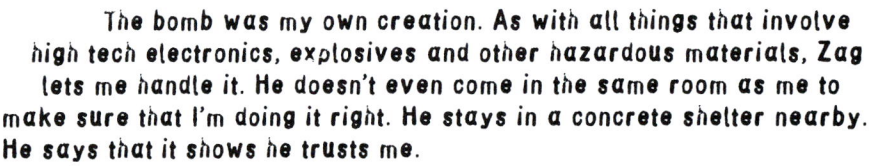

The bomb was my own creation. As with all things that involve high tech electronics, explosives and other hazardous materials, Zag lets me handle it. He doesn't even come in the same room as me to make sure that I'm doing it right. He stays in a concrete shelter nearby. He says that it shows he trusts me.

Yes.

I was pretty pleased with the bomb that I designed for the Pasquale job. It seemed to be quite suitable.

We got into the dressing room with the help of a monkey wrench and crow bar, planted the bomb and made a hasty retreat, bumping into Les Dennis on the way out. He was the compere for the award ceremony.
Unfortunately Les wanted the star dressing room, and so got Pasquale's.

Les Dennis became Les Miserables.

We bumped into Joe Pasquale, an un-blown-up, healthy-looking, about-to-get-an-award-and-very-happy-about-it-looking Joe Pasquale.

So we hit him.

It was our last attempt at getting rid of Pasquale. Even as we were fighting we heard the now-blown-up-and-not-very-happy-about-it-at-all Les Dennis announce the winner of the award. It was Frank Carson!!

I think it was rigged.

Zig, it wasn't. We were the ones trying to rig it. What happened was that Pasquale had won the award last year and you can't win it two years in a row.

And Carson didn't know, so we weren't going to tell him that it wasn't down to us. He was very happy.

Back in the office, I found that we had already spent most of the money, what with the Vegas trip, taking the babes out, the gambling ...

You said that the gambling was just a dream.

Em ... yes ... well ... I wanted to talk to you about that.

You!!!!!!!!!!!!!!!!!!!!!!!!

(EDITOR'S NOTE – *The Dirty Deed dictation goes very faint here as all that can be heard is punches, squeals and screams*).

Sorry about Zag's blood on the Dirty Deed dossier.

Dirty Deeds in History

Getting Eve to Bite the Apple

This was the first ever Dirty Deed.

Did Adam and Eve do the dirty deed or was it the snake?

Well actually Zig it was our great-great-great-great-great-great-great-great-great-great-great-great-great-great-great-great-great grandfather.

What was so great about him?

He was the man that had the first idea that you could make some good money from Dirty Deeding. He did come a little unstuck though when he found out that they hadn't invented money yet – so he had to be paid in fruit and vegetables.

Perhaps that's where I get my love of Broccoli! What did he have to do?

He dressed as a snake and asked Eve if she wanted a bite of the sacred apple.

Why?

Because she always wanted to go for walks in the forest with no clothes on and Adam wanted to watch the football on the telly.

The Trojan Horse

Another one of our ancestors, Toysareus Zag, came up with a brilliant idea of how the Tudors were going to defeat the Trojans.

Wait, wait, wait. Who was fighting who, why, where, how and when will I get my Broccoli milk shake?

After the Dirty Deeds in History lesson, now shut up. In the 5th Century the Tudors were fighting the Trojans because the King of the Tudors really fancied the Queen of the Trojans and he wanted to kidnap her. So our relative Toysareus Zag came up with this great idea. He knew that it was the Trojans' birthday and so he wanted to leave them a present of a wooden horse outside their city gates. Now inside this wooden horse was a man, all scrunched up, because a horse isn't very big and the Tudors were renowned for life-like sculptures. Well anyway, when the city of Troy was asleep this man would get out of the horse, unlock the gates and the army would run in and kidnap the Queen. That was the plan, but it went wrong.

What happened?

Another one of our ancestors, Hermeseta Zig, built the horse to the wrong measurements and instead of being one horse high, it was a thousand horses high. Luckily the Trojans were pretty stupid and brought the horse in anyway. Armies came out from inside and kidnapped the whole town.

The French Revolution

The King and Queen of France loved France, each other, but more than anything they loved cigars. But cigars are a bit rough at one end.

That's why you always see people biting the ends off in films.

That's right. So the King got an inventor that he knew, Charles De Gaulle De Zig, to come up with an invention that would help their cigar smoking enjoyment.

monsiEuR RobEzpiERRE Zag avec french babe

The cigar chopper was a big success. Such a big success in fact that they decided to build a big one that could chop the end off all the cigars at the same time. Unfortunately while the king and queen tried it out one day, they slipped and fell into the guillotine themselves and were beheaded.

And since there were no King and Queen the people of France decided to become a republic.

England Winning the 1966 World Cup

It was a time when England never had it so good. 1966. The swinging sixties!

Why was it called the swinging sixties?

Because anyone that was in their sixties had to swing on a trapeze before they could get their pension. It was part of an age old initiation ceremony that proved that they were getting on a bit. Unfortunately this practice has stopped recently – but I digress. England was in good spirits because the World Cup was being played here. All of the greatest football teams were in the competition.

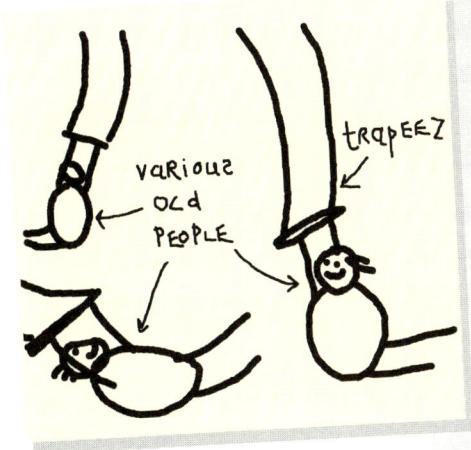

Was there a team from our planet, planet Zog?

No, we're not very good at football traditionally (although of course I am excellent), the reason being that our legs are only a foot long and we keep tripping over the ball. Also just having one toe means that we could break something when kicking the ball.

We're good at pancake tossing though on Zog.

Yes, unfortunately not a World Cup sport though, Zig. Anyway come the big final and Germany had a goal disallowed when they should have won against England! And why? Because the linesman was a Dirty Deeder!

ZIG AND ZAG'S DIRTY DEEDS FILE 003
"DESPERATELY SEEKING SWIMMING TRUNKS"

As dictated by Zig and Zag to secretary of the week, Miss Barren

MIGHT BE SECRET

Zig had really annoyed me ...

Sorry.

I had told him to never come into the office and mess about with my files ...

Sorry.

To never make any Dirty Deeds decisions without consulting his older and wiser brother ...

I've said sorry 47 times now.

But most importantly, to never, NEVER (I can't stress this highly enough), NEVER, sit in my chair.

Sorry, sorry, sorry. There, that's 50 times. Happy now?

No, Zig, I am not happy, but you don't have to keep apologising. I will simply stop your wages for a couple of weeks, until I believe that you have learnt your lesson.

You don't pay me anyway!

Well, perhaps I will pay you for the next couple of weeks, and just not give it you. That would teach you, wouldn't it? You see, dear Dirty Deeds Dossier, what Zig also did was hire a new secretary. Now I am not averse to a new secretary every week, in fact I'm all for it, and not in just some sexist way so that I can ogle different babes each week, no, I do it to help the employment figures. Anyway Zig hired a new secretary who with just one look could curdle ice cream.

She had good references and a very good CV.

Zig, her CV just said that she could make an excellent cup of Broccoli tea, and her references were from the Broccoli Tea Makers' Union.

Exactly!

I despair sometimes, I really do.

She proved very useful with Ken Moby, Zag.

Ken Morley, Zig, yes, she was. Ken Morley was our next Dirty Deeder. (For those of you that don't know Ken Morley, he's Reg Holdsworth from Coronation Street.)

The one with the wig, the strange eyes and the penchant for saying CHEESY!

Anyway he wanted a Dirty Deed done, and it was quite a nice one. He had left Corrie and wanted to open up a restaurant. Seeing the success of places like Planet Hollywood, he had decided on "Planet Reg."

PLANET REG

But of course, to succeed as well as its namesake, it too would need all the artefacts on the wall that keep the punters from thinking too deeply about what they are actually eating.

So I offered him some of our clothes, that's what I thought he'd come for.

One of the things that was going to make Planet Reg special though was that all of the artefacts on the wall were going to be famous people's undergarments. Not a bad idea in actual fact.

So I offered some of our pants.

But no, he didn't want those either.

He said they might put people off their food.

Zig's ↓

↗ Zag's

What he wanted was the swimming costumes of the team from Baywatch. Now, as you know, I have had a bit of a steamy relationship with a few of the cast from Baywatch in the past and just happened to have Pamela Anderson Lee's costume in my top drawer. I used to use it as a desk polisher.

I used to use it as a handkerchief.

Ken/Reg was extremely happy (almost delirious actually) that I had Pamela's costume. So after an exchange of cash, I handed it over, with the promise that we would soon get seven more: Michael Newman, David Chokachi, Alexandra Paul, Jaason Simmons, Yasmine Bleeth, Jeremy Jackson and Gina Lee Nolin.

Before we left I grabbed ahold of my new ZigCam (see separate pages of ZigCams) and offered one suggestion for Planet Reg. Perhaps if people eating at Planet Reg couldn't finish their meals, instead of a doggy bag, he could give them "food in your pants". A pair of pants with food in!

We left for LA at this point before Ken/Reg realised the kind of people he was dealing with.

Have you written to the airline yet?

What for?

There was some trouble with the seats on the plane, because Zag was sitting in the first class and I was in the cargo bay. It was very cold, in fact I had icicles dripping off my nose ... and I haven't even got one.

Yes ... I must write and complain. They ran out of champagne for me and Claudia Schiffer.

Huh? ... Champagne? ... Claudia Schiffer?

Em ... I was trying to get another Dirty Deed done. See if she wanted to do away with David Copperfield for once. I know I do.

I'd like to do the chopping in half trick with Copperfield, and then remember at the end that I forgot to do the trick part!

On the airplane I pulled the seat down to a bed ...

I was squashed between a pram and a rabid alsatian!

... and had a wonderful idea where by I could do a scam within a scam for the Baywatch Dirty Deed. I would need a van, some rope, a sack of disguises and a vast amount of expenses.

Zag didn't let me know what the scam was, but to be honest I couldn't really hear anything for the first day or so in LA, because my ear wax had frozen solid in the cargo bay. I did try to keep warm by breaking into a suitcase and putting on some of the clothes. Unfortunately the only case I could find was top TV personality Mike Smith's, and no-one in their right mind would wear some of the things in that case.

The only part of my scam that I couldn't find was a van, but Zig soon sorted that one out.

I pinched Lemmy's '70s custom-made van.

COPPERFIELD TRICK

blood 'n stuff

FILE THREE

Having done some research, like every good Dirty Deeder should, we found the nearest freeway and headed towards the Baywatch beach.

And like every other foreigner (and some native Angelenos) we got lost. Those freeways are amazing, we zig-zagged across five lanes of freeway looking for the right exit but we couldn't find any signs. The other drivers made it worse by beeping at us all the time.

I then pointed out to Zig that Americans drive on the other side of the road from us, and that we were driving the wrong way. Zig flipped a quick U-turn and we were chased by twenty or more cop shows.

It was like the OJ car chase. I wonder if he ever got prosecuted for that?

I then suggested that I drive, and we quickly found the beach. IT WAS RAINING!!

I couldn't believe it either. How could Baywatch be filmed here? Then Zag told me about Hollywood special effects, and how when it's raining somebody stands holding up a huge umbrella. They paint the inside blue with a few clouds and a yellow sun and bingo, it looks like Summer!

Michael Newman was found at the infamous Santa Monica Beach Gym working out, trying to stay toned for the Baywatch show. I told Zig to stay in the van and I would bring Michael over, then once we got Michael in the back of the van, Zig could whip his swimming trunks off and we would have one of the seven that was needed.

It said in my trusty Baywatch book that it was part of the Baywatch contract that the cast never take off their Baywatch costumes as they might be called day or night to be on set. Smells fishy to me!

Anyway I went over and chatted to Michael, told him about the ultra modern gym that I had installed in my new van and asked if he wanted to try it out. Michael fell for it hook, line and sinker.

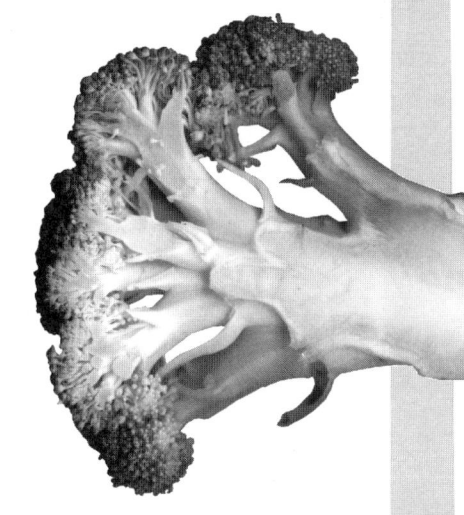

Once back at the van Zig managed to get the trunks off him and it was at this point that I had to tell Zig about my little scam within a scam. We were going to kidnap the Baywatch cast and sell them back to David Hasselhoff (not just the lead but the producer of the show) at the end of the Dirty Deed mission. It was not only brilliant it was clever.

I went along with it because I thought it would be very funny to have seven naked Baywatch stars in the back of the van!

Next on the list was David Chokachi. According to the trusty Baywatch book that Zig sleeps with under his pillow every night ...

I do not!

Chokachi could be found every night up in the Hollywood hills with a different babe. Sounds like a man after my own heart. He always did the same thing, take them up to the spot they romantically call Lovers Leap-on-my-bones, sit in his top-of-the-range convertible, talk to them about the stars, recline the seats ... then jump on them!

ZIG + ZAG'S DIRTY DEEDS DOSSIER
SHEET 40 OF 96

FILE THREE

ZIG + ZAG'S DIRTY DEEDS DOSSIER
SHEET 41 OF 96

FILE THREE

You're right Zag, it does sound like you. But you're not normally that subtle.

True, Zig. Normally babes just rip off my clothes whenever I get them into a romantic spot. Do you remember that night I had out with Analisa from Neighbours? I was taking her out because she was depressed about the possibility of getting dropped by the TV show. I had promised a night of passion at a secluded romantic parking spot. Well, I came home with my clothes in tatters. She jumped on me as soon as the car stopped. I wouldn't have minded but it was only at the traffic lights at Piccadilly Circus.

I remember the headline.

Yes. It was in the Guardian as well. However, I digress. Chokachi had the babe in the car, and we made our move. We pulled up in our van in front of him, shone the headlights into his car and we pretended to be LA Cops. Going exactly to my plan, he shielded his eyes from the light, and couldn't see who we were.

Which was a shame really because in the 2 hours that we had to wait, I had run up a couple of really nice police costumes.

Chokachi was taken back to the van for questioning, thrown in the back and stripped.

We had two, now for the third...

Jaason Simmons (yes he does spell his name like that, weird as it might be) was well known to feed his face at Cafe 50's in West Hollywood. That would be our next port of call.

I was pleased, I knew that they did the best Broccoli pancakes with a side order of Broccoli fries, this side of the Mississippi.

Another thing that was known about Simmons was that he was a keen philatelist.

ZAG! Don't be disgusting, you cannot say that! Children could well be reading this book.

Philately, Zigmund, is the study of stamps. And so no sooner had I let Simmons believe that we had one of the rare penny blacks in the back of the van, than we had Baywatch swimsuit number three.

I had fourteen pancakes and three helpings of fries, all washed down with an iced broccoli coffee.

Zig was then sick all the way to our next destination.

What was weird though was that it tasted as good going one way as it did the other!

Now who's being disgusting!

The last male was only half a man. In other words, it was the show's teenager, Jeremy Jackson. He was snowboarding out at Big Bear. My plan was to get him into the van, but how?

My idea was for Zag to pretend to hurt himself and to get Jackson to help him back to the van. A trick I learnt from Silence of the Sheep.

Silence of the Lambs, Zig.

No, Silence of the Sheep. I saw the old version! Ha ha ha ha ha ha ...

Very funny, Zig. But it wasn't a bad idea. It only needed one minor revision. Zig would obviously have to be the one that hurt himself.

Silence of the Sheep! Ha ha ha ha ha ha ha ha ha ha ha ....

Ha ha ha ha ha ha ha ha ha ha ha ......

Ha ha ha ha ha ha ha ha ha ha ha ....

Anyway we met Jackson at the top of the slope, ... and I pushed Zig down the slope. Jackson helped the bandaged Zig to the back of the van.

Sheep! Ha ha ha ha ha ha ha ha ha ha ha ha ha ha ha ha ha ....

Zig, you're getting hysterical now.

Now we had all four boys needed.

Ha ha ha ha ha ha ha ha ha ha ....

We'd have to get the girls next week ....
.... See "Desperately Seeking Swimming Trunks" part 2.

ZIG + ZAG'S DIRTY DEEDS DOSSIER
SHEET 46 OF 96

ZIG AND ZAG'S DIRTY DEEDS FILE 004
"STILL DESPERATELY SEEKING SWIMMING TRUNKS"

As dictated by Zig and Zag to secretary of the second week, Miss Barren

Last week we did this ....

MIGHT ALSO BE SECRET

All we had to do now was get the Baywatch Babes.

Can I ask a question?

Oh dear, here comes trouble.

What have you been doing since last week's Dirty Deed?

Well. It's been a busy week. Seven days means seven babes. Now don't ask me which one was which day, because I can't remember, but they were: Kate Moss, Sandra Bullock, Naomi, Cindy Crawford, Hilary Clinton, but that was actually for a Dirty Deed. She wanted us to help her with some accounts!

Madonna called up again every day, but after that trouble that I got into last time, I didn't think I'd risk it. Let's just say that thankfully the press is buying that story about who the baby's father is! What did you do, Zig?

Well Zag, first I cleaned the van, as I was told to. When I asked you what I should clean it with and you said "Use your head", did you actually mean Use my head?

No, of course not.

I thought not, I used my bum instead. It came up really shiny.

I can't see the van looking any shinier.

Not the van, my bum. It's so shiny you can see your face in it now. Take a look.

Zig, I am not going to look at your bum to see my face in it, thank you very much. Is that it, that's what you spent your free week doing in LA? Very exciting. Right, I can get on now can I?

That and being in a movie.

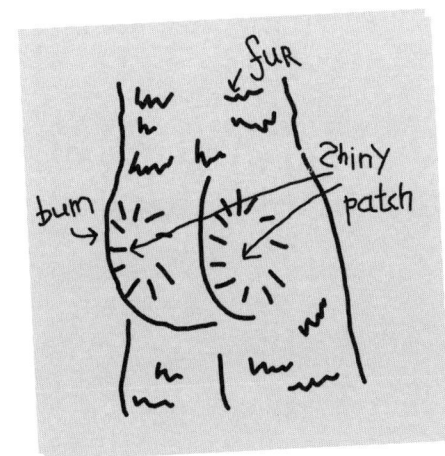

So, we had to start looking for the Baywatch babes. They would ....
Did you just say that you were in a film?

Yes, but no, carry on about the Dirty Deed. We must get this file done.

You were in a movie! How? When? Who? Why? Where?

Well I was walking down Melrose Ave, and I saw this little leaflet thing on a lamppost asking for people to be in a film.

I rang the number and went along for an audition. You know they say that thing about how in Hollywood people get their first job by getting on the casting couch?

You didn't sell your body to get a part in a film?

No, but I had to get on it, because the audition was to play one of the people in hospital in ER. I got the part because they said that they were looking for someone who looked like they had a very strange disease and I was perfect.

Zig, I don't think that was meant as a compliment.

So I went into the studio and I lay there all day while they were filming all of the stars doing their various bits ... but I started to get bored.

Oh dear, why do I get the feeling this is going to end up in some disastrous way?

ZIG + ZAG'S DIRTY DEEDS DOSSIER
SHEET 49 OF 96

FILE FOUR

So I went for a bit of a walk. But I was only wearing one of those hospital gowns, so I slipped on a white coat and a mask, so that no-one would recognise me and I wouldn't get into trouble.

But you did get into trouble, didn't you Zig? What happened?

Well. I wandered off set and walked straight onto the set of Jurassic Part 2. They were filming the scene where one of the dinosaurs is being operated on by some doctors ...

And they thought that you were one of the doctors. That's great! You're going to be in Jurassic Part 2!! Can I have your autograph?

Well I don't think I'm going to be in JP2, because I got a little carried away, and I cut the head off the dinosaur.

What!

And they threw me off the set, so I went back to ER, but they threw me off the set too.

Did they find out you had gone missing?

No. They didn't realise I'd gone at all. They threw me out after my big scene.

Your big scene?

Well George Clooney is supposed to come over and take a look under the blanket and say "Whew, this looks weird." Well, he came over, looked under the blanket and said **"Whew, hhuuuurgh!"**

Hhuuuurgh?

Yes, that's how you spell someone throwing up. You see, he threw up, because I had brought the head of the dinosaur with me, as sort of a memento.

And that's when they threw you off the set?

No. They loved it. They said it brought a certain "Godfather of the '90s" feel to the show. So they gave me a job as a writer on the show. They threw me off when I came up with this story about two aliens taking over the Emergency room and turning it into their American Dirty Deeds office.

.... Zig, you are unbelievable.

Then on the second day ....

Zig, I don't want to hear any more!

We had three more swimsuits to get to finish Ken Morley's request (See "Dirty Deed File 003"), and that was the rest of the babes. Grrrrrrrrrrr!:
1. Alexandra Paul.
2. Yasmine Bleeth.
3. Gina Lee Nolin.

Alexandra Paul was an old flame of mine. In fact I helped get her the job on Baywatch, but that's another story. I called her up and told her that I was in town, knowing she would want to see me straight away. I got her on her mobile, she was at a party, and she said it was very dull, that my being there would really liven it up for her. Unfortunately it was Lemmy's party.

**I'd found out that the van that I had stolen was Lemmy's.
I did this by several steps of deduction;**

**1) There was a greased pair of leather trousers in the back of the van.
2) Every single tape in the sound system case was of Motorhead. Everybody's face apart from Lemmy's had been coloured in.
3) And this was the thing that clinched it. Behind the dashboard was a sticker that said ...**

This van belongs to Lemmy
It is called Lilly
I've got a gun and I'm coming for whoever has taken her

ZIG + ZAG'S DIRTY DEEDS DOSSIER
SHEET 52 OF 96

FILE FOUR

ZIG + ZAG'S DIRTY DEEDS DOSSIER
SHEET 53 OF 96

GRRRRRR!

FILE FOUR

We managed to sneak into the party, and Alexandra was right. It was as dull as a very dull thing.

We sneaked in by dressing up as two preachers from the Reverend Church of Funk. One thing a rock and roll star will never do is leave a man of the cloth standing on the doorstep. They usually hit them over the head first.

Anyway, we got in and Alexandra Paul had been right. It was so-o-o dull. Jackson was just drinking tea, and Clinton hadn't started trying to chat up any women. I tried to get it going by suggesting a conga line, but only Flipper joined in, and he wanted to do an underwater conga.

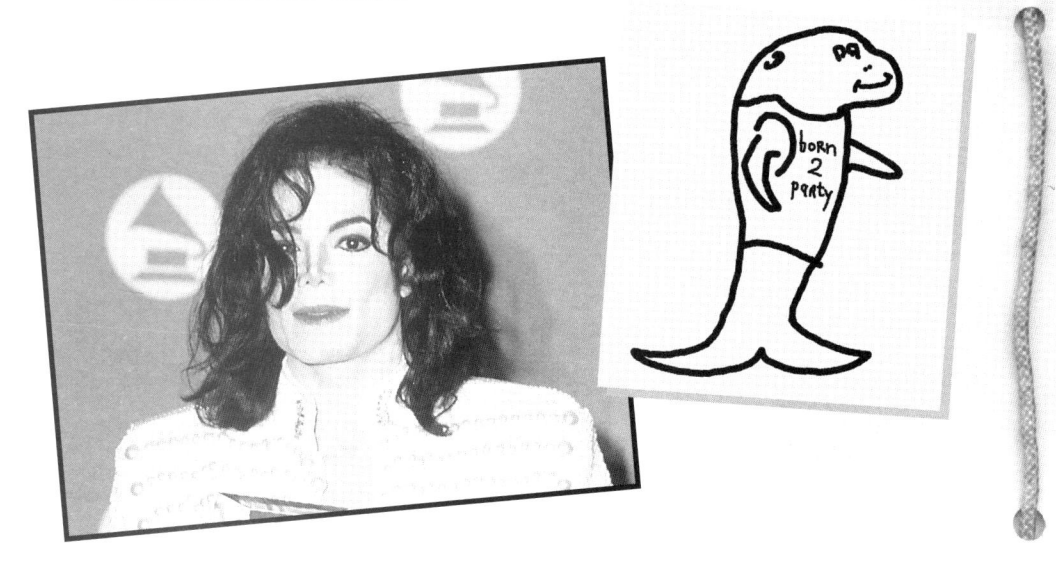

I spotted Alexandra Paul and sidled up next to her. After just a couple of sweet nothings whispered into her ear, she was putty in my hands. I told her that I had something to show her in the back of the van. She said that she'd already seen it, but wouldn't mind seeing it again . . .

5 swimsuits, 2 to go.

Yasmine Bleeth was proving to be a little trickier. We drove all over town trying to find where she could be.

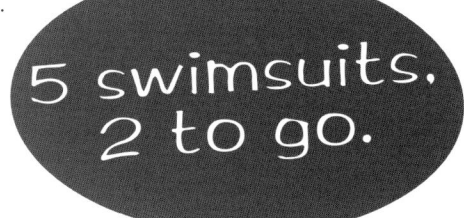

What we needed was one of those naff tours of Hollywood stars' homes. Then we could just jump off, knock on the door, badabing, badabum, and she would be in the back of the van. Here I made one fatal mistake. I let Zig get the tour. I thought there were only a few of these tours and they would all be the same. What did I know?

I picked the tour that had the coolest car. It was long, silver, sleek and silent. Really cool.

Zig, it was cool. In fact it was almost refrigerated. It was a HEARSE! Zig had booked us on Graveline – a tour of dead Hollywood.

Yeah, it was even cooler than I first thought. I saw the house that Bugsy Malone was shot in, I saw the homes of several murderers, and the places where lots of the living famous have become the dead famous.

Yasmine Bleeth, on the other hand, the person that we were looking for, was not dead, and our Graveline driver did not know where anybody alive lived. He did, however, know that Yasmine Bleeth was often to be found shopping in Melrose.

That's where I got the extra work on my second day as well. It was for a part in HOME ALONE 5 – "MCAULEY GET LOST!"

Sounds like a good film, but we don't want to know. Yasmine was found in a shop looking for some clothes for herself. Myself and Zig disguised ourselves as two typical LA boutique owners and helped her pick out some clothes. I fooled her into getting into the changing room to try something on, and while she was in there, I pounced.

6 swimsuits, 1 left.

According to my Baywatch book that I do NOT sleep with (well not every night, some nights I have my Coronation Street annual – I have a strange fascination with Vera Duckworth), Gina Lee Nolin was the only one left. And the book said that she very rarely left the set. So we whisked straight down there.

ZIG + ZAG'S DIRTY DEEDS DOSSIER
SHEET 57 OF 96

FILE FOUR

My first plan was to get Zig drowning in the waves, call for help, Gina would come out, I would trip her over and get her into the van. But that didn't work.

No, while I was drowning, no-one came to save me.

So the next plan was to get into Gina's camper van, and talk her into coming over into ours. I have to hand it to Zig, he managed it with a stroke of pure genius.

I set light to her bedspread.

She came to our van for safety!
We threw her into the back of the van, and that was it.

I immediately got on the phone to pay off my scam within the scam and sell back the naked captive Baywatchers to David Hasselhoff ... but he didn't want them!! Apparently they were all getting more fan mail than him, and so he said that he didn't care if he never saw them again. Zig and I got the swimsuits and ran.

Lemmy got his van with seven naked people in the back. So he was happy. It was like the '60s all over again.

Back at the Dirty Deeds office, Miss Barren (the weird secretary that Zig had hired) was trying to snog Ken Morley.

You're right, she was strange.

We gave Ken the swimsuits, he gave us the money and ran. We were happy for a while ... then we saw how distraught Miss Barren was.

She had fallen in love with Ken Morley. (She was absolutely Billy Bonkers, there's no question of that.)

I gave Miss Barren Ken Morley's address, for a slight fee of course, and Miss Barren left in a cloud of burnt shoe leather and cheap perfume.

Now that was cruel, Zag. He might never be able to get rid of her.

N.B.
Get in touch with Ken Morley. See if he wants a Dirty Deed done on Miss Barren.

Gosh, Zag, you're brilliant!

ZIG + ZAG'S DIRTY DEEDS DOSSIER
SHEET 60 OF 96

TOP SECRET!

DIRTY DEEDS WE'RE NOT ALLOWED TO SHOW

We got a call from John Major who had had a particularly embarrassing interview with Jeremy Paxman. He knew how Paxman lovingly coiffed his hair, and asked us to sort it out. Zig begged me to let him to do it.

Before Upside Down got us to get rid of BoyZone (see "DIRTY DEEDS FILE 005"), they had us get rid of Take That.

We knew that if we got to Robbie first and managed to convince him to leave then the others would break up soon anyway.

We hypnotised Robbie into thinking that he could sing!

He sounded like a cat with a hernia!!

UNSHOWN

ZIG + ZAG'S DIRTY DEEDS DOSSIER

At the end of Comic Collision (DIRTY DEEDS FILE 002) Frank Carson liked our work so much, he asked us to do one more. It was a big one.

He wanted us to make him funny.

That's not a Dirty Deed, that's a miracle. No, he wanted Bob Monkhouse, top comic with an encyclopaedic memory of comedy, out of the way.

We should have planted dynamite in his eyebrows. It would have taken years to find.

No, all we had to do was say, "'YES BUT HIS BOTTOM WAS BIGGER THAN BOB HOLNESS'S SISTER' IS THE PUNCHLINE TO WHAT JOKE?". Then sit back and watch his head explode.

What was the joke then?
There isn't one, that's what's funny.

You think that's funny! You've been watching too much Jim Davidson!

Our final unshown Dirty Deed is still too hush hush to tell you about, but let's just show you this, and see if you can take a wild guess.

UNSHOWN

ZIG AND ZAG'S DIRTY DEEDS FILE 005
"BATTLE OF THE BANDS"

As dictated by Zig and Zag to secretary of the week, Miss L'Amour

NOT VERY SECRET

You were snogging on the sofa, don't try kidding me.

Zigmund, I've told you umpteen times now. I was just helping Miss L'Amour look for her earring. She dropped it while sitting on the sofa and the two of us were groping around, looking for it.

Groping around is right. You were all hot and sweaty and you had lipstick all over your fur. Besides, you said that it was her contact lens that you were looking for.

Em ... it was ... a contact lens earring. They are all the rage in America, oh yes. You dangle your lens from your ear, so that you don't have to see anything that you don't want, and if there is something you do want to see, you just pop it in. It's very clever.

I suppose it would be good for seeing if you need to clean your ears out!

Happy now, can I get on with the dictation?

Sure ... I still don't believe you though. Why were you practically naked?

Ahem ... let's carry this on another time, shall we? Suffice it to say that I was with Miss L'Amour when you came into the office that morning. Which brings me to another point, why are you always late into the office?

Well, you know I was working on the new ZigAlarm clock?

ZIG + ZAG'S DIRTY DEEDS DOSSIER

Another brilliant invention? It doesn't work, you surprise me.

No, it does work. I'm quite pleased with it. Let me explain – once the little hand of the clock gets to the appointed hour then it pulls the string which lights the match, which in turn lights the candle. This heats the water in a saucepan. Once the water bubbles, it makes a sound which releases the sound activated dropper. This drops an egg into the pan which takes 5 minutes to cook. This ensures the egg is very hard boiled. An inbuilt catapult then fires the egg which bounces off my head, therefore waking me up!

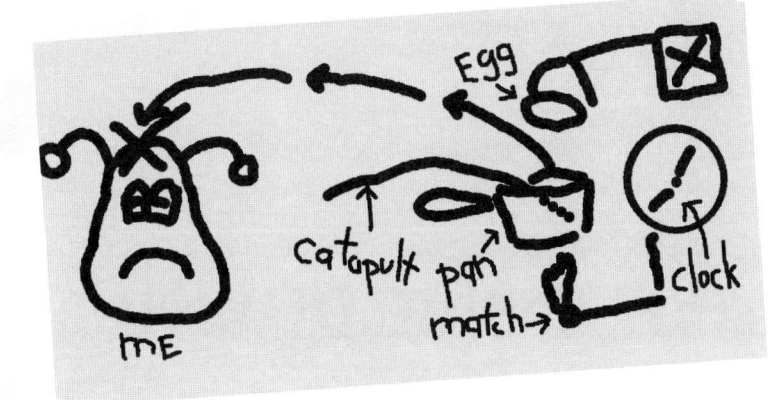

Sounds great. So what went wrong?

Well I have to get up fifteen minutes before it goes off, to set it.

I give up! Anyway, back to the Dirty Deed at hand. I, Zig and Miss L'Amour were visited by boy band sensation Upside Down ...

I don't know if people will remember them. They were big between May 15 1996 and May 16 1996. (Just the waking hours obviously, and not counting lunch or coffee breaks – so for about two hours all told!)

Zig! Don't be so rude. Upside Down have been very good to us. We've done two jobs for them. The Take That job (see "DIRTY DEEDS WE'RE NOT ALLOWED TO SHOW") and the BoyZone show, which we are supposed to be doing the file on, if I can ever get started.

Sorry! All I was saying was that Upside Down may not have been as musically gifted as say the Beatles ... or the Nolans.

N.B.
Ask Upside Down if they want a dirty deed done on Zig.

Upside Down had come back to see us for the second part of their Dirty Deed. We had sorted out Take That (see note above), and now all they needed was BoyZone out of the way, and they would be the top boy band in the country.

Excuse the interruption but aren't Blur, Pulp, Oasis, Radiohead, Dodgy, Lightning Seeds, Northern Uproar and Supergrass all totally male bands? Does that mean that Upside Down would want them out of the way too?

No, Zig, good idea though. Boy bands are the teeny bop bands, where the girls scream so loud that they can't hear what the band are singing.

Good job really.

Zig, a little word, there are a lot of girls out there who love these bands. These girls are in their teens where hormones race round the body and make them a little unsettled. Unsettled enough to attack anyone that takes the mickey out of them, or their family, but most importantly their fave band.

I see ... I LOVE UPSIDE DOWN!

That's better. We both love Upside Down – especially if their fans are around, or if they want another Dirty Deed done.

We don't love them as much as Miss l'Amour does. She was all over them: flirting, batting her eye lashes and whispering sweet nothings in their ears.

She was just keeping them happy. She didn't really fancy them, her heart belonged to someone else.

You're jealous! You were snogging her!!

SHUT UP, ZIG! I am not jealous, we were not snogging and she wasn't flirting with Upside Down.

No, of course she wasn't ... (he is jealous).

And don't do that. I've got a magnifying glass, you know!

(EDITOR'S NOTE – Please excuse the breakdown in the book. Zig and Zag will be continuing shortly – they just have to sort out a few technicalities. While you're waiting, here's some pictures of nature.)

(Ah, it seems that Zig and Zag are ready to continue now. Thank you for waiting – signed The Editor).

You hurt my throat!

So we had to get rid of BoyZone. My first plan was to get hold of their latest single and destroy it, so we went along to BoyZone's recording studio. To get in we had to pretend that we were in the music biz as well.

I designed some clothes and played about with some wigs. The result was

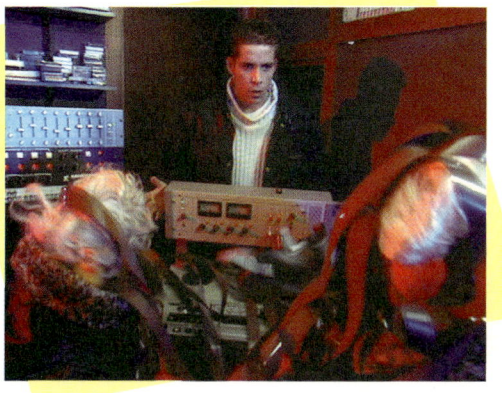

JODSON & RAMONE

We fooled the bouncer, got into the studio and ripped it apart.

When I came round we were outside.

I used my initiative. I ran away when Sean looked angry, and when I got back Zag was unconscious. I then learnt that BoyZone was doing a special appearance at a local girls' Primary school.

ZIG + ZAG'S DIRTY DEEDS DOSSIER

I was initially very pleased with Zig. I thought that he was starting to show real promise as a Dirty Deeder. Then I noticed what we were wearing!

It was the only way we could get into the crowd without getting noticed.

But we were noticed weren't we, Zig? Especially when you started screaming for Take That! We had to hide in the dustbins until the fans had run off.

But just think, if we hadn't been in the bins we would never have overheard that BoyZone were making a new pop video.

And I would never have had the smell of boiled Broccoli clinging to my fur for a week! That bin was disgusting.

That wasn't the smell of the bin. That was my aftershave, I poured it in the bin so that it wouldn't pong too much.

I don't want to hear this, Zig. From the bins we went to the video production office and listened in to the Director and the star.

The Director, Spat, was from the Belgian-Romanian borders (or that's what he said). He was well known as being a little outrageous, one of the reasons that he had hired Dani Behr to play a tree. I wanted to hear more about the video so that we could sabotage it, thus ruining BoyZone.

I suggested that we put a microphone in a cake and leave it in the room while they had their meeting. I didn't think they'd eat it!

No, of course not! It was a cake after all! I suggested putting a microphone on a nearby lamp – but that was seen as being too dangerous!
What happened when Spat and Dani ate the cake?

They died...

What? Sorry, didn't catch that.

They died. They swallowed the transmitters and choked on their own words. Okay? Happy now? I'm a failure!!!!

Don't say that, Zig. Thanks to my ingeniousness, I turned the potential disaster to our advantage. I became Spat, and Zig became my trusty cameraman Quentin Tagliatelly.

Notice my wigs and the clever disguise of my hidden camera as a video camera. (See "ZIGCAMS".)

We got in to see BoyZone and luckily they didn't recognise us.
My idea was to make the most ridiculous video ever made, thereby ridiculing the band and ruining them.

ZIG + ZAG'S DIRTY DEEDS DOSSIER
SHEET 68 OF 96

The song was called "Coming Home Now" and my idea was that they should all be coming home, but as different characters from History. I pitched them the idea .... and they fell for it! We made the video around Streatham, South London.

They thought we were going to be filming in Barbados, but I pretended that I got travel sick. They fell for that too!

THE VIDEO – COMING HOME

Director: Spat
Cameraman: Quentin Tagliatelly

Ronan played Hamlet, or "Omlette" as Spat would say.

Steve played "Clant Heystywoud" (Clint Eastwood)

Keith was a "specimen" .... (a spaceman)

Mikey was a "scooby doover" (a scuba diver)

And Shane was "Brave fart" .... (Braveheart)

FILE FIVE

The video was very funny. I thought it would ruin them.

It went straight to number one. Thanks to the old Ginger Whinger.

Chris Evans gave the video a rave, saying it was a "postmodernist statement on the values of Home. A brilliant satire. Pop videos will never be the same. Fabulous."

We just thought it was rubbish.

When we got back to the office Upside Down had gone and taken Miss L'Amour with them! (Don't say anything, Zig!) One good thing happened though ... Oasis asked us to direct their next video. I might do that one in the Bahamas!

Zag was upset that they took his girlfriend!

What are you saying? *Come here!*

(EDITOR – Sorry about this. Normal service will be resumed shortly.)

ZIGCAMS (BLUEPRINTS AND BLACK EYES)

Note here that the definition of ZigCam in the English Dictionary is:

ZigCam[1] *noun* a camera used in espionage by Zig, the dim and weird brother of the popular Zogly twins, Zig and Zag. (Zag's the most popular.)

Did I mention this is the definition in the **very rarely seen Zag's Concise English Dictionary and Conservative Charm Tips** – obviously not a very big book.

Get on with it, Zig. I only said you could have a couple of pages.

OK sorry.
The first ZigCam was the **GINGERELLA CAM**. I had designed it to be concealed in a normal pair of black glasses ....

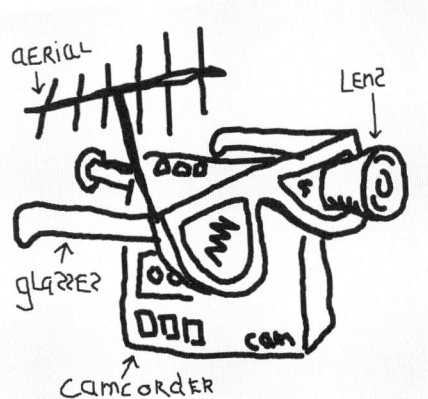

Only it was deemed a bit obtrusive, so I came up with this ingenious disguise for a ZigCam. I hid the secret camera within a real camera. No-one ever spotted it!

ZigCam 2 - The BLACKPOOL CAM.

This really was ingenious ... a camera hidden inside a piece of Blackpool rock.

Unfortunately I forgot and I ate it. So there's not much footage of that Dirty Deed!

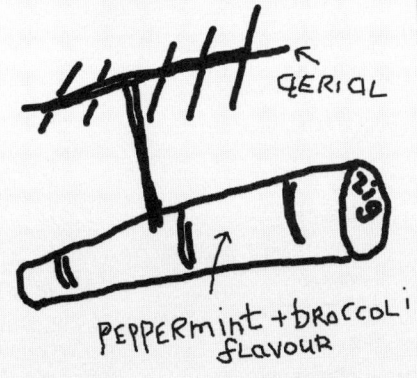

← AERIAL

PEPPERMint + bRoccoLi flavour

ZIG CAMS

ZigCam 3 and 4 were the same – CORGI CAM

I found a corgi ... well actually I picked it up when Zag did the Princess Di Dirty Deed ...

Shhh! We're not supposed to mention that.

Oh! You mean people think that she actually went out with Will Carling, and not that she was doing it to throw them off the Zag/Di scandal?

Shhhhhhhhhhhhhhhhhhhhhhhhhhhhhhhhh!!!!!

Okay, well anyway here's the corgi cam.

before   after

I was very proud of it!

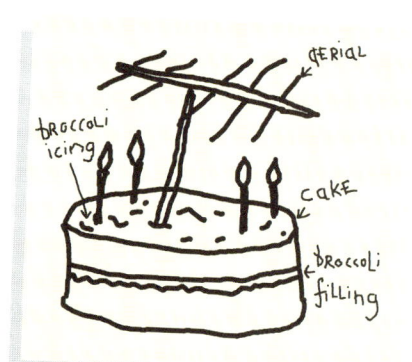

ZigCam 5 was the BOYZONE CAM.

Specially made to fit inside a cake. I don't know how they didn't see it.

Perhaps if they had, they wouldn't have eaten it, and not choked on it!

ZigCam 6 was my favourite.

Here's the BAGPIPE CAM. If you looked down one of the pipes, you could see what was going on.

Normally it was like Zag on a night after a curry – a lot of old wind!

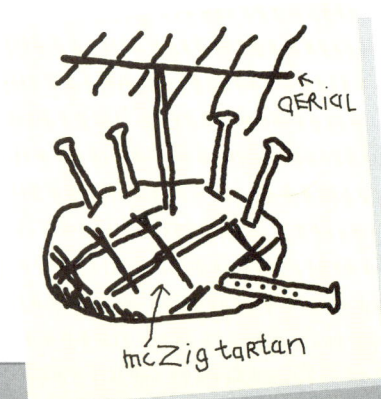

The final ZigCam was the most inventive. The **NEW YORK HAT CAM**.

We tried to make it out of an Empire State Building replica, but monkeys kept swinging on it.

ZIG AND ZAG'S DIRTY DEEDS FILE 006
"THIS PARTY SUCKS"

As dictated by Zig and Zag to secretary of the day, Miss Take

TOTALLY UN-SECRET

Time for a break. A holiday. Une vacance.

I think it is time for a holiday, you're starting to speak funny.

That is not strange. That's French. Une vacance means a holiday. (They better be pleased with this book. Not only is it funny, sexy (me), strange (you) and un-put-downable ...

Thanks to the superglue I put on the cover...

It is also informative. What other book gives you French while making you smile?

The French dictionary if you look up the word "BOTTOM".

La derrière. Do you think that's funnier than the English word for bottom?

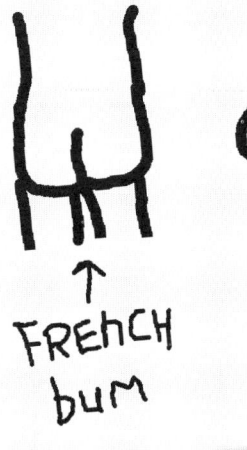

↑ French bum

↑ English bum

I think that an English bum is funniest.

Anyway we needed a holiday and so we decided to stop Dirty Deeding for the weekend and just relax. I thought possibly a couple of hours on the beach in St Tropez with my latest fling Sharon Stone, then on to Monte Carlo for a night of gambling, then perhaps a night-cap at my favourite penthouse suite at the Holiday Inn, Paris.

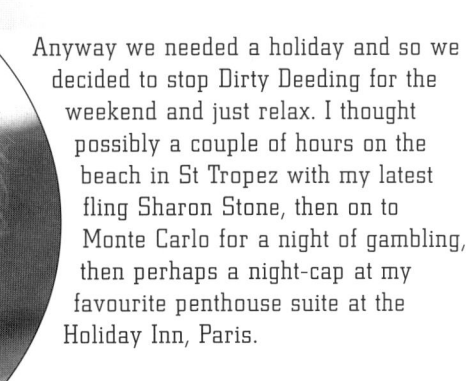

I fancied a weekend Broccoli picking in the Ukraine.

We couldn't decide. Then Lady Fortune smiled on us.

Is that John Fortune's wife?

We got a phone call from a mysterious, but strangely recognisable, voice. He invited us to his Scottish mansion for the weekend. He was having a celebrity party and so obviously wanted us with him.

Is a celebrity party like the Conservative Party but with recognisable people in it? (Political! Watch out, Ben Elton! Another couple of gags like that and the government will come tumbling down. There'll be anarchy in the streets. The Queen will get kicked out of her house and have to live on the streets like the kids. The stock market will crash, the world's finances will go haywire. America will panic and think that it's a Soviet plot. They'll push the button, the Russians will do the same. Total nuclear wipe out. ARMAGEDDON ... and all because I told a political joke.)

No Zig, all that will happen is that people won't laugh and you'll get grumpy saying "Well I thought it was funny".

Well ... I thought it was funny.

We decided to go along to the party. We got on the train up to Scotland ... and that's when things started to go really strange.

Yeah ... the train was on time ... we got empty seats and a clean table ... and - gasp, shock, horror - the buffet was open!!!

ZIG + ZAG'S DIRTY DEEDS DOSSIER
SHEET 76 OF 96

FILE SIX

ZIG + ZAG'S DIRTY DEEDS DOSSIER
SHEET 77 OF 96

FILE SIX

Stranger than all of that was that there was no-one else on board. And when we got off the train it seemed to disappear into the night. Just one hoot of the whistle and there it was ... gone!

No, I think the buffet being open was stranger.

We were picked up by Clutch, the manservant, and taken to Ochty McClochty on Tweed, to the house of our mysterious host.

NESSIE (artist's imprezzion)

It was quite a nice drive, we passed some great sights. I especially liked the little village of Dunfartin!

We passed Loch Ness on the way and it was all I could do to stop Zig from relieving himself into it. He said that if anything was going to get Nessie out of the water that would.
We were soon at the old manor house and it looked very scary.

But not as scary as the owner. It was none other than ...
   Jon Bon Jovi!

No, it was the one and only .... NICHOLAS PARSONS!

I nearly left there and then. I mean, can you imagine: you've had a twelve hour journey to a remote manor house with the promise of a celebrity weekend and then you find out it's Nicholas Parsons!

Nicholas showed us to our room, which apparently was haunted by a naked lady at midnight. I set my alarm clock and put on my best smoking jacket. I aimed to chat her up and see what transpired! I'd never kissed a spook before.

What about that woman from the Clothes Show. She's pretty spooky and you dated her for a while.

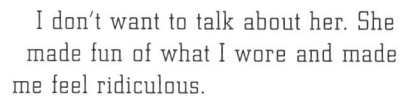

I don't want to talk about her. She made fun of what I wore and made me feel ridiculous.

That's terrible .... you don't need any help to feel ridiculous. I mean, look at what you're wearing.

And I suppose an anorak is any better. It's all I ever see you in. Don't you ever take it off to clean it?

Well, for your information Zag, I have 364 of them. One for every day of the year.

There's 365 days in a year.

I go naked on my birthday.

I shudder to think. Anyway, we were told by Nicholas that the meal that evening would be along the theme of horror ...

I dreaded to think what the food was going to be like.

He had selected some costumes and put them in the wardrobe, we got dressed and went downstairs. I went as Frankenstein.

And I went as Spock.

Zig, I meant to ask, can you tell me what's scary about Spock?

Well have you ever noticed that on Star Trek Spock never goes to the toilet. That's scary!

Em ... right. Thank you for that thought, Zig. I will now never be able to watch that TV show without thinking about that.

My only idea was that perhaps they have an outside loo.

outzide loo

We met the other guests at dinner. I was very pleased to see that they were all women. Jo Guest had come as Elvira, lady of the night, and Leslie Joseph had come as the Bride of Frankenstein.

I thought that Leslie had come in her own clothes!

Seldiy Bates was an actual Ghost Buster and Katie Puckrick came as the Monster that swallowed Birmingham.

Best thing for it really.

Nicholas himself had come as Dracula. We then sat down to eat a rather clever meal that Nicholas's chef had prepared.

You call sheep's eyes stewed in rats' vomit clever? I'm not eating anything that you cook ever again.

It wasn't real. He had made some gruesome looking dishes out of proper food.

Well then, why did everyone who tasted it spit it into their serviettes?

After the meal we went into the green room for coffee. I had a nice time chatting to the ladies.

Trying to chat them up, you mean. Meanwhile you leave me with Seldiy. She was a nutter. She kept telling me that strange things were going to happen and that I should be wary of people with teeth. That was everyone!

I also learnt something. The girls preferred Dracula to Frankenstein, so I'd picked the wrong costume. No one wanted to come for a midnight stroll.

Zag, it wasn't the costume, they just didn't fancy you. Leslie Joseph actually pushed you out of the way to go off with Nicholas Parsons.

ZIG, DO YOU WANT AN ANTENNAE TWEAK? NO? WELL SHUT UP THEN. I've told you before, Leslie was just going off with Nicholas because he was the host.

Later that night I woke up to the sound of a terrible sound. I thought it was someone cutting through flesh. It was a kind of sawing, screaming sound.

It was Zig snoring. You had snored so loudly that you woke yourself up doing it.

Well, why didn't I wake you up?

Because I sleep with cotton wool in my ears. I know how loud you can be.

I must remember that. Now I know when to call you all the things that I want to and not be worried that you'll hit me.

I wouldn't if I were you. I keep a tape recorder going next to me when I sleep, just so that if I think up any Dirty Deeds in my sleep I don't have to get out of bed to write them down.

You're very clever, Zag.

I know, Zig. Clever enough to know what to say to make you believe me.

Huh?

Nothing, Zig. Back to the celebrity weekend. In the morning over breakfast we found that Leslie had disappeared. She probably was so distraught that I didn't go knocking on her door in the middle of the night. Zig's friend Seldiy had also gone.

She was not my friend, she was Billy Bonkers.

Clutch the butler told us that the two had gone out early that morning. He also asked us if we fancied a little peasant shooting after lunch.

I thought that he meant pheasant shooting .... but no!

I managed to bag four of the blighters.

When we got back I decided to ring Zag Rent-a-costume, (another sideline), for a surprise for that evening.

I went for a walk and found Nicholas Parsons's bedroom. I was quite shocked to find that Nicholas has a very strangely shaped bed.

That evening at the meal I wore my newly acquired Dracula costume. I was determined to get off with one of the girls tonight. Unfortunately another one had gone, Jo, just leaving Katie as the only female.

In other words, another one of the girls had managed to give Zag the slip.

I hoped to get close to Katie after the meal, but I had used the wrong kind of mouthwash. I had used Zig's.

I had run out of Broccoli mouthwash, so had brought along that other favourite of mine, garlic flavour. It's always been lucky for me.

After dinner Nicholas suggested that we play a game, Blind Man's Buff. I agreed, perhaps I would find myself in some dark corner with Katie. Then I knew she wouldn't be able to resist me.

Is Blind Man's Buff where you get a blind man, strip him then try to pin a tail on him?

That's how we play it on our planet. No, Nicholas had some idea about us all being blindfolded ... but that was his plan.

Parsons was a real

VAMPIRE!

But we didn't know that. In fact when we took off the blindfold, we found Katie lying on the couch having been bitten, and I was blamed.

You were wearing the Dracula costume.

Zig, I'm your brother, you'd think that if I'd have been a vampire you would have known about it by now.

You never can tell. You do like to nibble a lot of girls on the neck.

Well, I was thrown into a cupboard, and through the keyhole I found out for myself what was going on. Zig was sent to the room to relax. Parsons then bit Puckrick ... and said that Zig was next. I escaped from the cupboard by my fake Vampire teeth, and headed upstairs to save Zig. Unfortunately I ran into some of our old friends. They were vampires too.

On the stairs I ran into the chef who came at me, hatchet in hand. I managed to get past him with a little side step and a big push.

Meanwhile I was upstairs in the bedroom thinking how cool it was that my brother was a prince of darkness, an undead dude.

I got there just as Parsons was about to pounce. There was a fight. Luckily for us the garlic aftershave did the trick. (Vampires hate garlic.)

Told you it was lucky.

Downstairs we got into the car to go home and I got onto the phone.

Ted Danson? What were you phoning him for?

He was on the lookout for a mansion up near Loch Ness. He had fallen in love with the place when he was filming.

You mean we were on a Dirty Deed all the time?

Zig, a Dirty Deeder never stops Dirty Deeding.

DIRTY DEEDS WE'D LIKE TO DO!

ZAG

1

Sort out the Charles and Di problem. Leave me alone with her for an afternoon, and she'll never want to look at another human again. That goes for Fergie and most other female royalty ...
... I draw the line at the Queen Mum though.

2

Get rid of the old guard of British comedy: Tarbuck, Forsyth, Corbett and Davidson. Easy though: just use exploding golf balls.

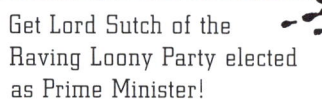

3

Get Lord Sutch of the Raving Loony Party elected as Prime Minister!

ZIG

1 — Get the Rolling Stones to do a concert from wheelchairs and Zimmer frames.

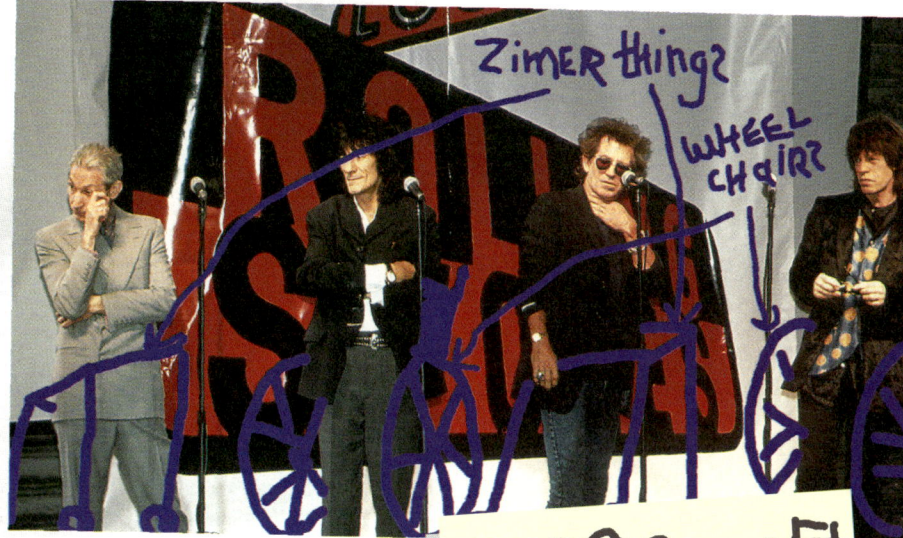

2 — Put a microphone in the Queen's toilet.

3 — The best ... get Delia Smith to do a whole book on Broccoli recipes.

ZIG AND ZAG'S DIRTY DEEDS FILE 007
"TO ELLE AND BACK"

As dictated by Zig and Zag to secretary of the week, Miss Disco Diva

QUITE SECRET (NOT)

This particular mission really did make me feel like 007. Saving a beautiful lady, having trouble with the police, getting tough with bad guys and still having the time to dance with a Disco Diva.

I liked this mission because I got to put you in prison. Ha, cool!

We're getting ahead of ourselves. Let me set the scene ...
It was a crisp morning, so crisp I expected it to rain salt and vinegar. The sky was blue, her eyes were red. Well, we had had a late night getting down at the Going Up, a new night-club where the glasses were dirty and the women were dirtier. I spotted the Disco Diva across the floor . . .

What are you talking about? Raining salt and vinegar? Are you feeling alright?

I'm just giving it the Sam Spade opening. I've always wanted to open a case like this.

Make up your mind: Sam Spade .... or James Bond?

OK, OK, I was in the Dirty Deeds office with the Disco Diva from the night before, we had danced all night, and weren't going to stop now. That's when Zig came in and we got the phone call. We were wanted in New York.

Was that a wig on her head or had she just put her finger in a socket?

The New York call was from an old friend, she needed help and so before she could say "Dirty Deeds" we were there.

Well that's not exactly true, is it, Zag? It takes seven hours on the plane, then there's immigration and customs. That's without taxis to and from the airport. I'd say all in all it would be ten hours door to door at the very least. That's an hour a letter – D.I.R.T.Y. D.E.E.D.S. Boy I'd hate to have a conversation with her.

Will you stop being so pernickety or do I have to zip your anorak over your head again, making sure that I catch your hair in it.

Sorry I spoke, stink breath.

We met the Dirty Deeder soon enough anyway. She looked great.

Does Elle McPherson have trouble in France? I mean "Elle" means "she" in French, she must get very confused, or should I say Elle gets very confused.

She wasn't getting in touch with us about troubles in France. She was getting in touch with us because she had troubles in New York. Someone had stolen pictures of her as a baby. Now apparently she was a very ugly baby and she thought that if the world saw her ugly, they might not want to see her again.

Well that's just stupid. People like baby pictures, it doesn't matter if you're ugly. People just say "aaaaah" no matter how you look. I mean you weren't a particularly handsome baby, look ....

Don't show that pho–........

I mean look, you've got the kind of face only a mummy could love.

And you're going to have the kind of face that a plastic surgeon would love to get his hands on, if you show any more pictures.

The only other photo that I have of you is that photo of you during your punk phase.

Don't you DARE show that photo.

.... Maybe

Let's just get to the Dirty Deed. Elle gave us a list of suspects that she thought might have taken the photographs, and the reasons why.

These were the four main suspects.

Uber Babes **PM Dawn**  **Dog Eat Dog**  **Lords of Brooklyn**

What about all the millions of ugly people?

She didn't have enough paper I guess.

← some ugly people

We jumped into the Dirty Deeds cab and off we went. The first suspects on the list were the Uber Babes – a group of models who aren't quite in the supermodel league.

The equivalent of Brighton and Hove Albion to Manchester United.

Brighton and Hove Albion have got some pretty crazy fans, Zig.

Not that Brighton and Hove Albion aren't a great team, they are, I'm not disputing that. It's just that Manchester United are the best.

Now you've upset every other fan, Zig. I'd quit while you still have some chance of being able to walk with two legs.

Not that Man Utd are that great. I mean if it wasn't for Cantona ...

Zig, at least you still had the Man Utd fans. Now you've got no-one except Cantona on your side.

Well, if there's going to be a fight, I'm with the right one then!

Zig, come here ....

Sorry about that, Zig, but the gag is on for your own safety.

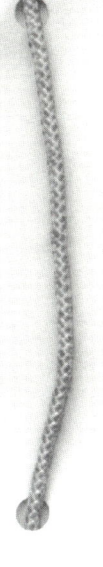

Where was I? Ah yes, the Uber Babes. Myself and Zig managed to infiltrate the gym and ask some questions. I got a date, Zig got a black eye, but we both didn't get any information about Elle's photos.

Mmmnjjdn mkmiiiijnn mmdnnmmnjnnnm.

I think Zig said that he could have beaten her in the fifth round. Pity she knocked him out in the first really. Our next suspect was PM Dawn, he was at his night-club. Apparently Elle was supposed to go into partnership with him, but she backed off at the last minute. We managed to get past the line outside the club by saying that we were Disco Police and that we had heard that they were playing terrible music.

Mmmnkk Mmnya.

That's right, Zig. "Like Enya." Inside the club wasn't really jumping, not until Zig got behind the console, then it really rocked.

I had no luck with PM Dawn, except that I learnt that in NY it's cool to call everyone "dog". So after I left the Chihuahua we went back to the hotel room to regroup and rethink our strategy. Didn't we, Zig?

Mjbkjh
kghsfilughflkhb
kjhfdkluhasdlfkuh
kjhdfkluhas
nmnbmbk
mnbkjhgju kjbnkhk nm,nkhkhk m,n,jhkjh
  jhfiuh8dfuy jkhgfhjlhsb hbisughfoasyg mjbfiuhfipuhqwp
    jaghfipuhaflajk kjhfkuh ljhf iuhgbiug l ig igigyg
  ygygljugi giukjh;piugpiuh kjhiughpg kjbhiugpgpiugh
  kgkljhvjv hjvjhvjjkh,jhvbjklhg jhgv jhjlhb ljhuyguygofbv
  asa aa a sdffdf

What?

MNBMDBGMB GMDNBGMSB MNBMGHJKBG MNBMBJKBM MBMB MNBMBM ....

Alright, alright I'll take your gag off. Now what did you say?

I said "Yes". You asked if we went back to the hotel and I answered yes.

All that mumbo jumbo was just "Yes"?

Well the editor wants 96 pages, I thought it might help.

Any more cheap gags like that and I'll gag you again.

If you gag me again I'll show that photo of you as a punk.

OK, we're even.
Next day we got up nice and early because we had to catch Dog Eat Dog while they were playing Basketball. Apparently Elle used to go down to play with them every morning when she was going out with the lead singer.

ZIG + ZAG'S DIRTY DEEDS DOSSIER

We played a little game with them, but Zag had the best shot of the day. He hit a policeman on the head. I also liked the way you ran off down the road, chased by the policeman and screaming for your mummy.

Zig! ....

A, a, a, remember I've got that punk photo.

So you have. Yes, I did run down the road screaming for Mummy, if you must know, but I did run straight into the pool hall where our last suspects were. It had to be them.

We talked ....

......they threatened .....

.... we backed off.

I wanted to stay and fight but Zag chickened out.

Rubbish. Zig, it was your mouth that he's holding in that photo, it was you that was whimpering with pain ...

Now where did I put that photo ....

What am I saying? I must be going mad. Of course I remember now, it was me that was scared and you wanted to fight.

I thought you'd remember properly if I jogged your memory. It was just after that that the policeman found you and carted you down to the police station.

Yes, my dear brother Zig came down and was told to pick the person that threw the basketball out of the line up. Now obviously I didn't want him to pick me out ... but ...

**... well you were the only one that I recognised. I got on the phone to Elle/she and told her all about it.
She told me about a planned money drop the next day. I had to find out who it was that had the photos and in the meantime she would get Zag out of jail.
I waited up all night and watched the drop off point. It wasn't long before I saw the man pick up the money. I chased him. We ended up outside a hotel off Time Square.**

ZIG + ZAG'S DIRTY DEEDS DOSSIER
SHEET 94 OF 96

I followed him in and up to the penthouse suite. I burst in the room and confronted the villain.

It was Ru Paul! Apparently she was jealous of all the attention that Elle was getting and she (not Elle/she but Ru Paul/she) wanted to be the top model in New York. She started crying and I felt sorry for her, so I promised not to call the police. She thanked me, told me I was cute and asked me out on a date. I don't usually go out with girls but there was something different about Ru Paul.

I'll say. Zig, do you know who Ru Paul is?

A very glamorous model, who fancies me, not you. Maybe I should go out with her just to make you jealous. Maybe we would fall in love, and get married, that would be a big surprise for you, wouldn't it Zag?

Yes, but not as big a surprise as you'd get.

Well I saved the day and went back to Elle and gave her the photos.

I had got out the night before, but had to rest up at Elle's place. I gave Elle a kiss goodbye and we left, but not before I managed to get my hands on Elle's negatives.

Two days later I was back in the office dancing with the Disco Diva ...

... and I was out in the market selling Zag's latest brainwave: "The Elle McPherson Ugly Baby Calendar".

And that is that. The last of the Dirty Deed files for now ... Who knows who will be the next person to have a Dirty Deed done?

It could be this person ...

I'm going to KILL YOU!!!!!

ZIG + ZAG'S DIRTY DEEDS DOSSIER
SHEET 96 OF 96

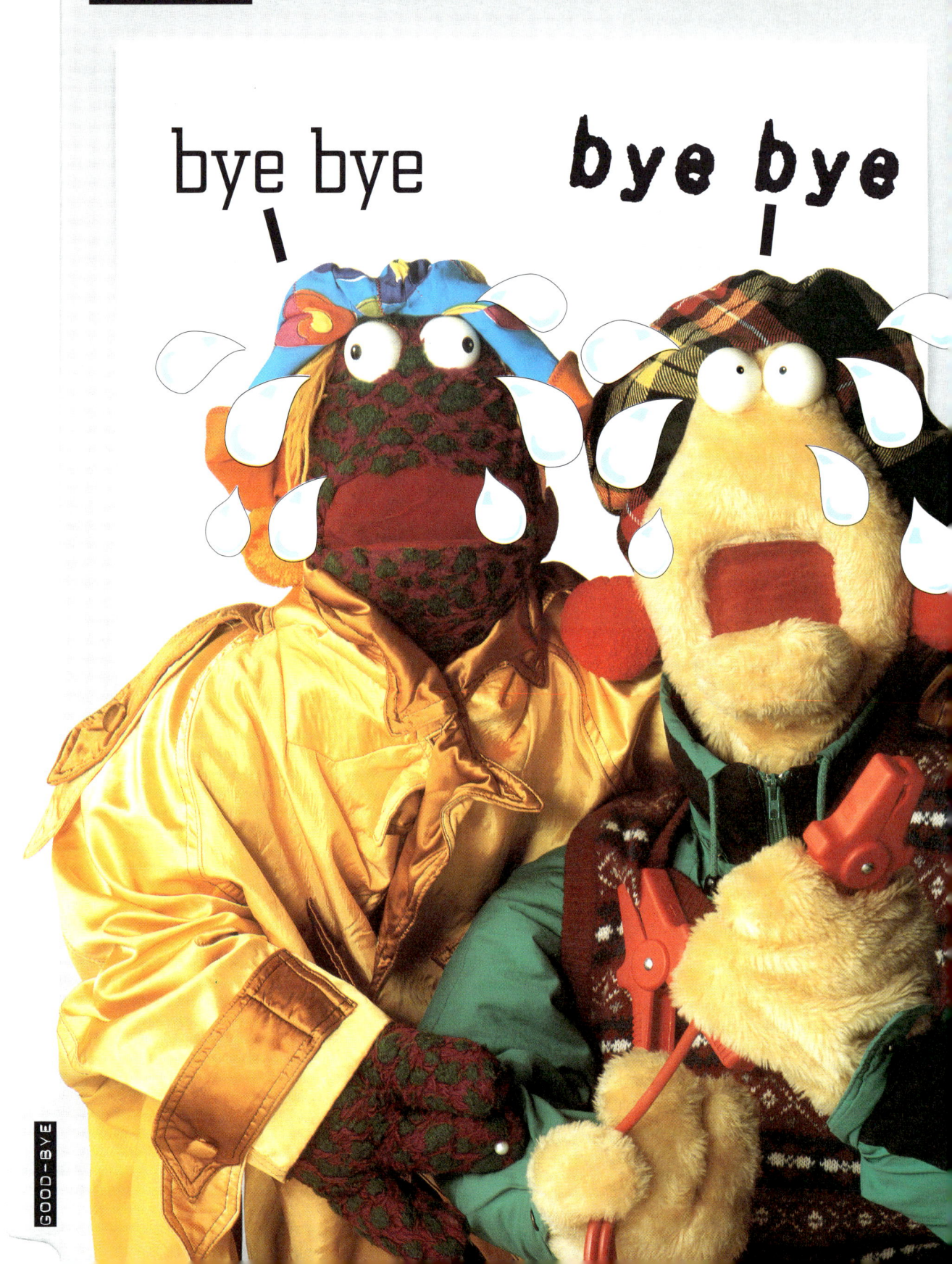

bye bye bye bye

GOOD-BYE